# WATER STORIES FROM THE BIBLE

**Stories of the Living Water and the Invitation in God's Word for All to Come and Drink**

*Revised Version*

**"With joy you will draw water from the wells of salvation" Isaiah 12:3.**

**J.O.Terry**

Church Starting Network

## Other Resources from
## Church Starting Network

### Church Starting and Growth

### English

Daniel R. Sánchez, Ebbie C. Smith, and Curtis Watke, *Starting Reproducing Congregations: A Guidebook for Contextual New Church Development.* Ft. Worth, Texas: Church Starting Network, 2001.

Daniel R. Sánchez, Ebbie C. Smith, and Curtis Watke. *Starting Reproducing Congregations Strategy Planner: A Workbook for Contextual New Church Development.* Ft. Worth, Texas: Church Starting Network, 2001.

Ebbie C. Smith, *Growing Healthy Churches: New Directions for Church Growth in the 21st Century.* Ft. Worth, Texas: Church Starting Network, 2003.

Daniel R. Sánchez & Rudolofo González. *Sharing the Good News with Our Roman Catholic Friends.* Ft. Worth, Texas: Church Starting Network, 2004.

Daniel R. Sánchez, *Gospel in the Rosary.* Ft. Worth, Texas: Church Starting Network, 2004

Ebbie C. Smith. *Spiritual Warfare for 21st Century Christians.* Ft. Worth, Texas: Church Starting Network, 2005.

Daniel R. Sánchez, ed. *Church Planting Movements in North America.* Ft. Worth, Texas: Church Starting Network, 2007.

Daniel R. Sánchez, *Hispanic Realities Impacting America: Implications for Evangelism and Missions.* Ft. Worth, Texas: Church Starting Network,

Ebbie C. Smith, *Basic Churches are Real Churches.* Ft. Worth, Texas: Church Starting Network, 2009

ii

## Spanish

Daniel R. Sánchez, Ebbie C. Smith, and Curtis Watke, *Como Sembrar Iglesias en el Siglo XXI.*

Daniel R. Sánchez, Ebbie C. Smith, and Curtis Watke, *Mis Planes Estratégicos Para Sembrar Iglesias en El Siglo XXI: Libro de trabajo para el desarrollo contextual de una iglesia nueva.* Ft. Worth, Texas: Church Starting Network, 2002.

Daniel R. Sánchez & Ebbie C. Smith, *Cultivando Iglesias Saludables.* Ft. Worth, Texas: Church Starting Network, 2008.

Daniel R. Sánchez & Rodolfo González. *Comparta Las Buenas Nuevas Con Sus Amigos Católicos.* Ft. Worth, Texas: Church Starting Network, 2004.

Daniel R. Sánchez. *Evangelio En El Rosario.* Ft. Worth, Texas: Church Starting Network, 2004.

Daniel R. Sánchez. *Iglesia: Crecimiento y Cultura.* Ft. Worth, Texas: Church Starting Network, 2004.

Daniel R. Sánchez. *Manual para Implementar Crecimiento y Cultura.* Ft. Worth, Texas: Church Starting Network, 2004.

Daniel R. Sánchez. *Realidades Hispanas Que Impacta A América: Implicaciones para Evangelización y Misiones.* Ft. Worth, Texas: Church Starting Network, 2006.

J.O. Terry, *Guía Para La Narrativa Bíblica* (Synopsis of the Bible Storying Handbook, translated into Spanish by Keith Stamps). Ft. Worth, Texas: Church Starting Network, 2008.

iii

# Bible Storying Resources

J.O Terry, *Basic Bible Storying*. Ft. Worth, Texas: Church Starting Network, 2006.

Daniel R. Sánchez, J.O. Terry, LaNette Thompson. *Bible Storying for Church Planting.* Ft. Worth, Texas: Church Starting Network, 2008.

J.O. Terry, *Bible Storying Handbook: For Short-Term Church Mission Teams and Mission Volunteers.* Ft. Worth, Texas: Church Starting Network, 2008.

J.O. Terry, *Guía Para La Narrativa Bíblica* (Synopsis of the Bible Storying Handbook, translated into Spanish by Keith Stamps). Ft. Worth, Texas: Church Starting Network, 2008.

J.O. Terry, *Hope Stories from the Bible.* Ft. Worth, Texas: Church Starting Network, 2008.

Daniel R. Sánchez and J.O. Terry. *LifeStory Encounters*. Ft. Worth, Texas: Church Starting Network, 2009.

J. O. Terry, *Death Stories from the Bible*. Ft. Worth, Texas: Church Starting Network, 2009.

J. O. Terry, *Food Stories from the Bible.* Ft. Worth, Texas: Church Starting Network, 2009.

J. O. Terry, *Grief Stories from the Bible.* Ft. Worth, Texas: Church Starting Network, 2009.

J. O. Terry, *Water Stories from the Bible.* Ft. Worth: Church Starting Network, 2009.

*The Church Starting Network supplies all of these resources:*

*www.ChurchStarting.net*

*3515 Sycamore School Road, Fort Worth, Texas 76133*

The stories are prepared for use by those who go to provide access to the needed clean water for the hopeless thirsty living in a dry and parched land, or where the waters are polluted leading to disease and death.

And who, in addition, offer good news of the source of Living Water to the spiritually thirsty so they might be satisfied, healed, cleansed of their sin, and given life and hope.

# WATER STORIES FROM THE BIBLE

© **J. O. Terry**
July 2000 Original Edition
July 2009 Revised
J. O. Terry

*Water Stories from the Bible* are adapted from stories as presented in the New International Version Bible. The stories as presented may be used as models for local versions, or adapted and translated as needed to meet the need with different people groups.

ISBN 978-0-9825079-9-5

# WATER STORIES

# WATER STORIES

## Foreword

I had never thought much about water until we lived in the Philippines. Our first house, in the outskirts of Manila, was in a subdivision that had its own well. The water was not chlorinated and soon the pipes coming into our house were filled with algae and had to be dug up and cleaned out. Further, the water pressure was low and required a pump at each house to boost the pressure.

I still remember one evening during our first week in Manila when we were having supper with the older missionary I was appointed to work with. His wife was explaining to us new missionaries that she boiled all their drinking water just to be safe. As she was saying these very words I saw her kitchen helper filling the ice trays from the tap at the sink!

Yearly mission meeting times were the times for many in the group to get bad tummies from the water. The water where we met was from deep wells. But the ice used was brought in from a local municipal ice plant.

In later years in Manila we had moved up into the city proper. The city water was dependent on a reservoir that was not able to supply enough water for a thirsty metro area of some ten million people. For this reason, many times the taps were dry. At other times, the water supply was so limited that we rationed our water and literally bathed from jars of water. Some had powerful suction pumps to pull water from the lines, but these often pulled pollution from ground water into the aging rust-pitted pipes.

When I went out to an area where I was also serving as an evangelist-church planter, I visited in the homes of the farm people. There was usually one of four choices for drinking when thirsty. One was warm bottled drinks which are very sugary in that country. Another was a hot cup of coffee with about a tablespoon (or more) of brown sugar in it. Another choice was to drink a coconut if you could find one. And the last was the water offered by the family from their container.

I recall one home in which I was often invited to visit with the family and take rest between our Sunday services. I had inquired about the water from their container that they assured me came from a deep well. One day as we happened to walk from their house through a swampy area to the church, we passed a pit in the dry creek bed. There was evidence that buffaloes had often gathered in that place. The family member casually mentioned as we passed by pit that it was their "well." That ended my drinking their water!

In that country it is impolite to eat or drink something in the presence of others without offering to share it. I used to long for the time when the last service was finished down in a rural area Sunday evening and I could get in my car to head home. Under the front seat was a thermos of cold water. But to my dismay, almost every time one or more people offered to "accompany" me back into town. All I could think about was that cold water just a few feet away waiting for me, but not enough to share!

There were many adventures with wells when I first began telling the Bible stories in South Asian countries. I quickly learned that many wells in Bangladesh were either salty from being near the sea, or polluted with fecal bacteria from toilets located near the shallow wells in sandy soil. Other wells contained arsenic from mineral deposits in the ground. I still remember the night I was bathing at an arsenic-polluted well and accidentally swallowed some water and regretted it for several hours afterward.

The location of our Bible Storying camp depended on the local wells that were not good for drinking due to either salt or arsenic. So a water man was employed to bring water from a deep well that had good water. He brought several large barrels each day. But as it turned out, the clean water from a deep well had "no taste" so the people in our camp complained. The next day they said the water had a better taste. But by that evening we were all sick with diarrhea. It turned out that the water man had stopped by the roadside and scooped up some ditch water to add to the clean water to give it a better taste. I had medicine with me for the diarrhea, but by a second week water-borne hepatitis made life miserable for the next two months.

In India we had little iodide resin filter cups to carry with us when we traveled to rural areas. In spite of using these one would still manage to get *giardia* or an occasional amoeba. But the most fascinating wells were those that had concentrated iron dissolved in the water. The wells were deep. The water was cold when it came up. But it was a milky yellow color. When the water was left standing for about thirty minutes, the water would turn red like tomato juice as the iron in the water oxidized from the air. The taste was, well, very "irony" and difficult to drink even after filtering.

In some of the rural areas we had encouraged the people to construct sand filters in barrels. The iron-laden water after it had oxidized was the consistency of a thick red soup. It was poured in the top of the barrel over the sand. The filtered clear water came out the bottom. The people were amazed that "dirt" made water clean!

Once when on a small island in the Philippines all the people bathed in the sea. However, I had taken a bar of a certain brand of locally sold soap with me. In salt water the soap made a rubbery residue on the skin and in the hair. It was terrible. There was no clean water on that island.

All drinking water was brought over by boat from a nearby island that I happened to visit. That day I noticed a dead chicken that had fallen into the well which was really only an open dug cistern and not very deep at that. That night I came down with high fever and diarrhea which I suspect was cholera *el tor* which each year kills many children due to dehydration from the diarrhea. I was so sick that night and many times had to run to the beach as there were no toilets on the island. I survived but it was a terrible ordeal from bad water. Unfortunately it was an all too common ordeal for people living the island.

As I recount all these experiences it reminds me of the wonderful gift of clean pure water to drink and to use for bathing. How precious it is. How wonderful when it is abundant to quench one's thirst.

A colleague who visited north Kenya told of seeing dug wells a hundred or so feet deep that people climbed into down steep stairways dug into the sides to draw their water at the bottom. The wells were controlled by the predominant major religion in that area and one had to profess that religion to have access to water in that dry thirsty land.

An anecdotal story I heard told of a friend visiting a missionary in a certain South African country. One morning the friend had gone out early to watch the local women working in their fields. As they worked the women were singing a song with a hauntingly beautiful melody. The friend listened for some time and then her curiosity got the best of her. She went to the missionary and said, "Come out here and listen to these women singing as they work. What are they singing about in such a beautiful song?" The missionary listened for a minute or two and then said, "The song goes like this: If you boil the water, the children won't get diarrhea!" The song had been used to remind the women so their children would remain healthy. Water-borne diseases are very prevalent in many Third World countries, especially during their monsoon times or where their community water sources get polluted through ignorance and carelessness.

It was said that Lottie Moon, an early missionary to China, was called a "devil woman" in Pingtu where people believed that if she used a well it would become polluted. Belief like this is common in several Asian countries where a higher caste or predominant religion controls the wells and prevents others from using them lest they pollute the wells.

In Bangladesh the local mission had projects to sink shallow wells in villages that had no wells or wells with bad water. In Cambodia there was also arsenic in the ground water so

4

the mission there worked on simple technology using sand filters and ultraviolet light to purify surface water for drinking. In some parts of India the custom was to dig wells, sometimes up to fifty or more feet deep through soil and sometimes granite.

In one place I had gone to visit in the Philippines the village was up on a ridge. The water the villagers had been using came from a river down in the valley below. Daily the villagers trudged up and down the hill carrying water for their homes. The mission had begun a project to sink a well for them in their village. I observed how the local people would gather around to watch a well team sink a well. This usually required only a couple days in Bangladesh in their sandy soil with water near the surface. In other places a week or so was needed because the wells were deep or had to penetrate rock. People watched and waited for the moment when clean water was produced. I realized that these people would be a captive audience for stories.

As I looked beyond the traditional long Bible Storying strategies we were using in the villages, I also saw a potential for shorter more compact Bible Storying opportunities during clean water projects. The Bible had many water stories that could be used during this time to entertain the people, to engage the people in how other people longed for water to drink, and to begin presenting the water of salvation to those who were not only physically thirsty, but who lived in a spiritually dry land.

To answer this need, the series, *Water Stories from the Bible,* was compiled and began to be shared among those who had water projects. As word spread about the collection of stories many requests came from other parts of the world.

For short projects there is generally not enough time to tell all the stories unless the stories are fast-tracked one after another until all are told. It may be that *The Water Stories* would only ignite an interest to hear more stories beyond the project when a team member might return to tell additional stories selected for more aggressive evangelism. Where local churches have sponsored water projects they have been encouraged to continue telling the Bible stories after the well team finishes and departs.

A new use for *Water Stories from the Bible* has emerged during disaster response for situations like the tsunami that struck the Indonesia area several years ago. In disaster areas clean water for drinking often has to be brought in and distributed. So whatever the situation, where there are any projects related to water, it should be appropriate to tell *Water Stories from the Bible*.

There are companion story sets. One is *Hope Stories from the Bible* that deals with God's providence and care during times of disaster. It is for use during disaster response and relief ministry. The other is *Food Stories from the Bible* for famine relief and feeding programs that shares Bible stories about God's provision for food, eating, hunger and fasting, feasts, and the living bread that satisfies spiritual hunger.

All three of these story sets have an evangelistic drift that is subtle and so can be used even where there is hostility to traditional more direct evangelism. The first intent is a loving and compassionate ministry to hurting, thirsty, or hungry people. The background intent is to begin leading listeners to consider that God is powerful to help us in our great need. Also the intent is to tell that beyond our daily bread there is spiritual bread that satisfies our hungry souls, and a drink of living water that quenches the deepest spiritual thirst and bubbles up to salvation within.

I share these stories as a suggested resource to use or a model to encourage the local development of appropriate water stories.

I lived in Asia for thirty-three years working among peoples in East Asia, Southeast Asia, and South Asia. My primary assignment was broadcast media. I had a growing interest in a more reproducible people-powered media that could be introduced locally by a person and allowed to penetrate a people group. This led to an interest in using Bible Storying as a strategy to evangelize and plant churches, and for training newly emerging leadership among oral leaders. *Water Stories from the Bible* was motivated by a desire to take advantage of every opportunity to share God's Word where people were gathered around water projects forming a potential listening audience for Bible stories leading to eternal life and planting a New Testament church among the people.

May the Lord richly bless each water project storyer and give wisdom as these stories are shared among thirsty listeners.

# WATER STORIES

## Introduction

In the following section of this book is a set of suggested stories in which water, sources of water, thirst, bathing, and baptism are the themes. The stories have been adapted from many of the well-known biblical stories and references. Some of the stories are compilations of scripture passages and joining of one or more stories to make one composite narrative with a theme related to water.

Only a set of basic Scripture References are given along with some additional references used later in the stories. The user should feel free to adapt any of the stories as needed to make them more appropriate for their listeners. It is realized that the stories will be either translated or modeled from these stories. It may be necessary to add additional introductory thoughts for the stories, or to add comment in the stories to clarify things for listeners or to answer their questions after telling the stories.

Some of the stories have strong evangelistic themes, some do not. Some are perhaps more entertaining for the listeners. This does not, however, reduce their value in authenticating the Scriptures for the listeners or in the morals or lesson themes embedded in the stories.

In teaching from the Bible there are two basic approaches—one is *embedded truth* in which the teaching points are embedded in a story and the story is kept intact and uninterrupted* as a story carrying its message.

The other is *extracted truth*—that which is extracted from the story and usually expressed as discussion points that are listed and may or may not be explained by exposition. In the worst case scenario the integrity of the story is abandoned and only the extracted points are expressed with a passing reference to the story as the source. Another

9

scenario is to begin telling the story, interrupt the story whenever a teaching point is reached, and explore the point before moving on with the story.

These first two scenarios are very disturbing to oral communicators. The third scenario when using extracted points is to at least tell the story, keeping it intact and uninterrupted and then, if one must, extract the teaching points for explanation or lead the listeners in discussion of the story and its meaning to facilitate *their* discovering the truths.

If a full storying lesson is desired, then familiarize yourself with the stories and think about questions to ask and issues to discuss with listeners before telling the stories that will stir their interest in the stories, and will sensitize them to the story truths. Some storyers may need to read from the Bible a portion of the story or one of the key passages in the story. Do this before telling the story. A read story can allay fears that one is changing the Bible by only telling the stories. But a told story provides for oralizing a story for telling so that it is easy for listeners to receive, understand and remember.

For post-story discussion, think about some factual questions regarding the story to be sure listeners understood the story. Then consider some "what if" or "think about it" questions to help position listeners in the story or otherwise relate listeners to the story. Finally move on to some questions like: What does this story say to you? What new thing have you learned from this story? What should you now do after having heard this story?

One might simply say, "Let's talk about what you've heard." Let the listeners process the story with their comments and questions. A story talked about is a story remembered. This exercise will help to move toward some personal application for the listeners.

It is good to review or retell previous stories, or even have one of the listeners try to recall the story if they can. Most oral communicators enjoy hearing stories over and over. Take every advantage of their immediate interest in water and the water project.

Each time you use the Water Stories take note of any questions that may be asked by the listeners and especially if these same questions come up often. You may want to work something into your session that will either head off the questions or will serve to put to rest those commonly asked questions.

It goes without saying, but I'll say it anyway—Pray about each story that the Holy Spirit will put a thirst in the listeners' hearts to desire the Living Water of Salvation from Jesus.

These stories represent a form of *Point-of-Ministry* Bible stories that relate to an event or a ministry opportunity. If there is interest, it is good to move the listeners over to a fuller strategic Bible Storying approach which deals more completely with Old Testament themes leading to an awareness of sin and its consequences, and the Gospel stories about the possible forgiveness of sin and salvation through faith in Jesus. Your listeners may need to know more about their accountability to God, their helpless predicament as sinners in God's sight, and the mercy God has shown by sending Jesus to suffer and die for sinners and then raised to life again as a promise of the believer's resurrection.

See the section at the end regarding **Telling the Stories** for a fuller account of things to consider when opportunity arises to share *The Water Stories from the Bible*.

*\* Some brief interruption (or inserted comment) may be necessary to explain some unusual reference in the story that would not be familiar to the listeners and which may either be crucial to the meaning of the story or add to its perception and interpretation in some way.*

**Note**: *Scripture references in quotations and italicized are there for the storyer's reference or in case an interpreter needs them but not necessarily to be quoted while telling a story. For most listeners among oral communicators this would only be meaningless words that interrupted telling the story.*

11

# WATER STORIES

## 1. In the Beginning
## God Created the Seas

*Bible Reference:* Genesis 1:1-28; 2 Peter 3:5

Long ago, according to the Word of Creator God, the heavens existed and the earth was formed out of water and with water. This is how it happened:

In the beginning when God began creating the heavens and the earth, the earth was shapeless and empty, and there was only darkness. The Spirit of God was hovering over the waters that covered the earth.

God said, "Let there be light." Light appeared. God was pleased with the light and called it "daytime" and the darkness God called "nighttime." So there was evening and morning of the first day.

Again God said, "Let the water vapors separate to form the sky above and the seas below." This happened on the second day. God said, "Let the water beneath the sky be gathered into seas so that dry land will appear." God named the dry land "earth" and the waters "seas."

On the third day God said, "Let the earth burst forth with every sort of grass, seed-bearing plant and fruit trees with seeds inside the fruit, so the seeds will produce plants and trees after their kind."

Next God said, "Let there be lights in the heavens to give light to the earth, the sun to rule over the day and the moon to rule over the night. God also made the stars. God saw that it was good. This was done on the fourth day.

Again God spoke saying, "Let the waters of the earth be filled with fish and living creatures. And let birds of every kind fill the skies. God looked at his work with great pleasure and blessed the creatures he had made. "Let your numbers increase, fill the seas and fill the skies," God said. This happened on the fifth day.

On the sixth day God said, "Let the land produce living creatures of all kinds, livestock, wild animals and creatures that move along the ground." God saw that His work was good. Then God said, "Let us make man in our image, in our likeness, and let them rule over the fish of the sea, the birds of the air, over the livestock and over all the earth and the creatures that move along on the ground." So God blessed the man and woman He made and said for them to have many children and descendants. God was very pleased with his work. On the seventh day God was finished with all his creation. So the heavens and the earth and the seas were completed.

The psalmist said: *"By the word of the Lord the heavens were made. He gathers the waters of the seas into heaps and puts the deep seas into storehouses" (Psalm 33:7). "God gave the sea its boundary so the waters would not overstep his command"* (Proverbs 8:29).

God is the maker of heaven and earth, the sea and everything in them.

———

*Come, let us sing for joy to the LORD; let us shout aloud to the Rock of our salvation...For the LORD is the great God, the king above all gods...The sea is his, for he made it, and his hands formed the dry land* (Psalm 95:1, 3, 5).

# WATER STORIES

## 2. God Provided Water
## For the Garden

*Bible Reference:* Gen 2:4-15; Psalm 65:9-10

When the LORD God made the earth and the heavens, no shrub of the field had yet appeared on the earth. No plant of the field had yet sprung up. At that time the LORD God had not yet sent rain upon the earth. Streams came up from the earth and watered the whole surface of the ground.

After the LORD God had formed a man and breathed into him the breath of life, the man became a living being. The LORD God planted a garden in the east, in Eden, and there the LORD God placed the man He had made.

A river watering the garden flowed from Eden, and from there it divided into four streams and passed through the lands where there was gold, precious stones, and fragrant spices.

The LORD God had made all kinds of trees grow out of the ground—trees that were pleasing to the eye and good for food. The LORD God commanded the man saying: "You are free to eat from any tree in the garden, but you must not eat from the tree of the knowledge of good and evil, for when you eat of it you will surely die."

The LORD God took the man and put him in the garden to work it and care for it. It was after this the LORD God made the first woman.

Sometime later the serpent tempted the woman saying, "Did God really say, 'You must not eat from any tree in the garden?'"

The woman said, "We may eat fruit from the trees in the garden. God did say, "You must not eat fruit from the tree that is in the middle of the garden or you will die."

When the serpent assured the woman that it was all right to eat of the tree to become wise like God, she did take some fruit and ate it and gave fruit to her husband who also ate. So they disobeyed God's command.

At this time the man and woman became ashamed and afraid and hid themselves when they heard God calling. Because they disobeyed God now they would die and their bodies return to dust, they must now work to grow their food. The woman would give birth to children in pain while her husband ruled over her.

Sin had entered the world and it would now spread to all descendants of the first man Adam and first woman Eve with serious consequences for all peoples.

———

*As the rain and snow come down from heaven, and do not return to it without watering the earth and making it bud and flourish, so that it yields seed for the sower and bread for the eater, so is my word that goes out from my mouth: it will not return to me empty, but will accomplish what I desire and achieve the purpose for which I sent it* (Isaiah 55:10-11).

# WATER STORIES

## 3. The Great Flood
## When God Judged the Earth

*Bible Reference:* Gen 6:1-9:17

When the descendants of Adam and Eve began to increase in number on the earth the LORD God saw their great wickedness. Every thought in the hearts of the people was evil all the time. When the LORD God saw this happening He was grieved that He had made man and his heart was filled with pain. So the LORD God said, "I will destroy mankind, whom I have created, from the face of the earth—men and animals, and even the creatures that move along the ground and the birds of the air. For I am grieved that I have made them." The people on earth had greatly corrupted their ways.

But the man Noah found favor in the eyes of God. Noah was a righteous man, blameless among the people of his time, and he walked in a way pleasing to God.

God said to Noah, "I am going to put an end to all people for the earth is filled with violence because of them. So prepare an ark (or boat) with cypress wood. Make rooms in it and coat it with pitch inside and out. Put a door in the side and an upper, middle and lower deck. When I bring floodwaters on the earth to destroy all life, I will make a covenant with you to save your wife, your sons and their wives. You are to bring a male and a female of every living creature into the ark to keep them alive. And of the clean animals you are to bring seven pairs. You are to take every kind of food that is to be eaten and store it as food for you and the animals." Noah did everything just as God commanded him.

At last the ark was finished and God spoke to Noah, "Go into the ark, you and your whole family. Take with you the

17

animals and creatures as I have commanded. Seven days from now I will send rain on the earth for forty days and forty nights until I destroy every living creature I have made."

Noah obeyed God. After Noah and his wife, his sons and their wives and all the animals and creatures had entered the ark, God closed the door. When seven days had passed it began to rain. The springs of the great deep burst forth and the floodgates of the heavens were opened. The waters rose until the whole earth was covered, even the highest mountains. Noah and those with him were safe from God's judgment inside the ark. Every living thing with the breath of life that moved on the earth died—birds, livestock, wild animals, all the creatures that swarm over the earth, and all mankind.

After the waters had flooded the earth one hundred fifty days, God remembered Noah and those with him in the ark. God sent a wind over the earth and the waters began to dry up. Noah sent out a dove that returned in the evening with a freshly plucked new leaf in its beak. Then God said to Noah, "Come out of the ark, you and your family. Bring all the animals, birds and creatures out so they can multiply and increase in number."

Noah offered a sacrifice that was pleasing to God. After God had blessed Noah and his sons He commanded them to replenish the earth with their descendants.

God said, "I will establish my covenant with you: Never again will all life be destroyed by the waters of a flood, never again will there be a flood to destroy the earth. This is the sign of the covenant I am making you and every living creature, a covenant for all generations to come: I have set my rainbow in the clouds. When I bring clouds over the earth and the rainbow appears in the clouds, I will remember the everlasting covenant between God and all the creatures that live on the earth."

*It was by water also that the world of that time was deluged and destroyed* (2 Peter 3:6).

*The Lord is not slow in keeping his promise...He is patient with you, not wanting anyone to perish, but everyone to come to repentance* (2 Peter 3:9).

20

# WATER STORIES

## 4. Redigging Stopped Up Wells

*Bible Reference:* Genesis 21:22-34; 26:6-33

Not many years after the great flood that covered the earth during the days of Noah, a man named Abraham lived. Abraham who was a descendant of Noah lived in a far away country with his father and brothers. While still a young man the God of heaven called Abraham to leave his father and his people and to go to a land that God would give to Abraham and his descendants. Abraham faithfully obeyed what God told him to do. There God had promised to bless Abraham, to make his name great, to give him many descendants, and one day through one of Abraham's descendants God would bless all people on earth. But Abraham and his wife had no son and they were getting old.

God did bless Abraham as He had promised and one day when Abraham and his wife Sarah were both very old, God fulfilled his promise to them by giving them a son named Isaac. During those days Abraham had also become very wealthy with great numbers of cattle and sheep and servants. To provide water for his animals Abraham had his servants to dig wells wherever the animals went to graze.

There were other peoples living in the land at that time who had lived there a long time. One of these was a king named Abimelech. Earlier Abraham had met Abimelech when the king coveted Abraham'd wife Sarah to be his wife. When the king took Sarah, God spoke to him in a dream one night saying, "You are good as a dead man because of the woman you have taken." When Abimelech realized his mistake he returned Sarah and gave Abraham many more cattle and sheep as well as more servants and a large sum of money. So Abimelech said to Abraham, "My land is before you; live wherever you like."

After some time passed Abimelech and his commander came to Abraham and said, "God is with you in everything you do. Swear to me that you will not deal falsely with me or my children. Show to me the same kindness I have shown to you." And Abraham agreed. Then Abraham complained to Abimelech about one of the wells of water that Abimelech's servants had seized. But Abimelech said, "I don't know who has done this. You did not tell me, and I heard about it only today."

So Abraham brought sheep and cattle and gave them to Abimelech and the two men made a treaty. Then Abraham set apart seven ewe lambs from the flock. When Abimelech asked Abraham, "What is the meaning of these seven ewe lambs you have set apart by themselves?" Abraham replied, "Accept these seven ewe lambs from my hand as a witness that I dug this well." So that place was called Beersheba, or the well of the oath, because it was there the two men made a treaty over the well.

Later in the days of Abraham's son Isaac, while he was living in the land and also was very wealthy with many flocks and herds, the servants of the neighboring Philistines envied him. So all the wells that his father Abraham's servants had dug, the Philistines stopped up, filling them with earth. Then Abimelech king of the Philistines said to Isaac, "Move away from us; you have become too powerful for us." So Isaac moved away from there and camped in another valley and settled there. Isaac reopened the wells that had been dug in the time of his father Abraham that the Philistines had stopped up after Abraham died. Isaac gave the wells the same name they had before.

Then Isaac's servants dug in the valley and discovered a well of fresh water. But the other herdsmen quarreled with Isaac's herdsmen and said, "This water is ours!" So Isaac gave that well a name that means "dispute." Then his servants dug another well, but there was a quarrel over it also, so Isaac named it "opposition."

Isaac had built an altar and worshiped the God of heaven that blessed him and promised to be with him. Then Isaac's servants dug still a third well, and no one quarreled over it. So he named that well Rehoboth which means "room," saying, "Now the LORD has given us room and we will flourish in the land." King Abimelech and his commander again came to see Isaac who asked him, "Why have you come to me, since you are hostile to me and sent me away?" And the king and his commander replied, "We saw clearly that God was with you and how He has blessed you. Let us make a treaty so you will do us no harm just as we did you no harm."

So Isaac made a feast for King Abimelech and his commander. After Isaac had sent them on their way his servants came and told him about the well they had dug. They said, "We have found water!" So Isaac named the new well Shibah (Sheeba) which means "oath."

In the day of Isaac abundant water was scarce and precious. His servants had to dig for it and there were people who could come and stop up the wells. It would be one of Isaac's descendants who would provide abundant water, Living Water, which no one could stop up the source or take away. That descendant was Jesus, the one who came from God and offered the Living Water to all who would freely receive it.

———

*Jesus said, "If a man is thirsty, let him come to me and drink. Whoever believes in me, as the Scripture has said, streams of living water will flow from within him"* (John 7:37b-38).

*To a woman Jesus said, "Whoever drinks the water I give him will never thirst. Indeed, the water I give him will become in him a spring of water welling up to eternal life"* (John 4:14).

# WATER STORIES

## 5. Stories from Around
## The Springs and Wells

*Bible Reference:* Genesis 24:1-24, 57-67; 27:41-46; 29:1-13; Exodus 2:11-22; 18:3-4

Many of the stories from the Old Testament part of God's Word take place where there was water. For water is necessary to life. And where there is water, people and animals must go to quench their thirst.

---

The first story is about a man whose prayer was answered by a drink of water. Isaac, the son of Abraham, was now a man. His mother had died and Abraham wanted to get Isaac a wife from among his own people. So Abraham sent his trusted servant Eliezer with ten camels and many gifts back to the land of Abraham's relatives. The servant made his way to the town and had his camels to kneel near a well outside of the town. It was toward evening, the time when women go out to draw water.

Then the servant prayed: "O God...give me success today... See, I am standing beside this spring, and the daughters of the townspeople are coming out to draw water. May it be that when I say to a girl, 'Please let down your jar that I may have a drink, and she says, 'Drink and I'll water your camels, too'—let her be the one you have chosen..."

Before the servant had finished praying, a girl came who was very beautiful. She went down to the spring and filled her jar and came up again. The servant hurried to her and said, "Please give me a little water from your jar."

"Drink, my lord," the girl said and quickly lowered her jar to her hands and gave the servant a drink. After she had

25

given him a drink, the girl said, "I'll draw water for your camels too, until they finish drinking." So she emptied her jar in the water trough, and ran back to the well to draw more water, and drew enough for all his camels.

When the camels had finished drinking, the servant took out a gold nose ring and two gold bracelets. When he asked whose daughter she was, she said, "I am the daughter of Bethuel, the son of Nahor." Nahor was the brother of Abraham. God had led the servant to the right place and answered his prayer with a drink of water. Later the girl Rebekah returned with Abraham's servant and became the wife of Isaac.

————————

The next story is about Jacob the son of Isaac. Jacob had cheated his brother Esau out of his birthright and then deceived his father Isaac into giving the blessing intended for Esau to him. Because of this, Esau was thinking to kill his brother Jacob. But his mother learned of the plan and said to her husband, "If Jacob marries one of these local Canaanite girls like Esau has done, my life will not be worth living." So Isaac agreed it would be good to send Jacob back to his relatives to find a wife.

When Jacob came to the land of his relatives he saw a well in the field with three flocks of sheep lying near it because the flocks were watered from the well. The stone covering the mouth of the well was very heavy. When all the flocks were gathered there, the shepherds would roll the stone away from the mouth of the well and water the sheep. Then they would return the stone to its place over the mouth of the well.

Jacob asked the shepherds, "My brothers, where are you from?"

"We are from Haran," they said.

Then Jacob asked, "Do you know Laban, Nahor's grandson?"

"Yes, we know him," the shepherds replied.

26

Then Jacob asked, "Is he well?" "Yes, he is," the shepherds said, "and here comes his daughter Rachel with her father's sheep."

"Look," Jacob said, "the sun is still high; it is not time for the flocks to be gathered. Water the sheep and take them back to pasture."

"We can't," the shepherds replied, "until all the flocks are gathered and the stone has been rolled away from the mouth of the well. Then we will water the sheep."

While Jacob was still talking with the shepherds, Rachel came with her father's sheep, for she was a shepherdess. When Jacob saw Rachel, daughter of Laban, his mother's brother, and with her father Laban's sheep, Jacob went over to the well and rolled the stone away from the mouth of the well and watered his uncle's sheep. Then Jacob kissed Rachel and began to weep loudly. He told Rachel who he was, a relative, so Rachel ran to tell her father. Later Jacob married Rachel and also her sister Leah. But it was Rachel that he loved, the one he met at the well.

---

The third story is one from some years later from the days of Moses. Moses was born in Egypt during the days when the ruler of Egypt had decreed that all the boy babies among the Israelites were to be thrown into the river to die. Moses' life had been spared when his mother placed him in a reed basket and put him in the river. There he was found by the king's daughter and raised as one of the king's own sons.

But one day when Moses had gone out to where the Israelites were working, for the Egyptians had made them slaves, Moses saw an Egyptian beating an Israelite. He was filled with anger and killed the Egyptian. When the king heard what had happened, he sought to kill Moses. But Moses fled from the king and escaped from Egypt and went to a place called Midian where he sat down by a well.

A priest of Midian named Jethro had seven daughters, and they came to the well to draw water and fill the troughs to water their father's flocks. Some shepherds came along and drove the girls and their sheep away, but Moses came to the girls' rescue and watered their flock.

When the girls returned to Jethro their father, he asked them, "Why have you returned so early today?"

They answered, "An Egyptian rescued us from the shepherds. He even drew water for us and watered the flock."

"Where is he?" Jethro asked his daughters. "Why did you leave him? Invite him to have something to eat." Moses agreed to stay with the man, who gave his daughter Zipporah to Moses in marriage. Later Zipporah gave birth to a son and Moses named him Gershom (*alien there*), saying I have become an alien in a foreign land. Later Zipporah gave birth to another son and named him Eliezer (*God is my helper*), for he said, "My father's God was my helper; he saved me from the sword of Pharaoh king of Egypt."

———

*With joy you will draw water from the wells of salvation* (Isaiah 12:3).

*Oh LORD...all who forsake you will be put to shame. Those who turn away from you will be written in the dust because they have forsaken the LORD, the spring of living water* (Jeremiah 17:13).

# WATER STORIES

## 6. God Divided the Sea
## To Deliver Israel

*Bible Reference:* Exodus 7:19-21; 14:8-31

When God called Moses to deliver the Israelites from bondage of slavery in Egypt, God sent Moses to Pharaoh the king of Egypt. "Let the people go," Moses said to Pharaoh. But Pharaoh would not obey the words of God spoken by Moses. Pharaoh hardened his heart. So God said to Moses, Go to Pharaoh in the morning as he goes out to the water. Wait on the bank of the River Nile to meet him, and take in your hand your staff. Then say to Pharaoh, 'The LORD God has sent me to say to you: Let my people go so they can worship me in the desert. But until now you have not listened. By this you will know that I am the LORD. With the staff in my hand I will strike the water of the river and it will be changed into blood. The fish in the river will die and the river will stink. The people will not be able to drink its water.'"

So God said to Moses, "Stretch out your staff over the waters of Egypt—over the streams and canals, over the ponds and all reservoirs—and they will turn to blood. For blood will be everywhere in Egypt, even in wooden buckets and the stone jars." Moses did as God commanded and all the water in Egypt was changed into blood. The fish in the river died and the water smelled so bad that the Egyptians could not drink it.

But Pharaoh again hardened his heart, he would not listen to Moses. Instead, Pharaoh turned and went back into his palace and did not even take this matter to heart. The Egyptians had to dig alongside the river to get drinking water because they could not drink the water of the river.

Again and again God sent Moses to Pharaoh to ask him to let the Israelites go. But Pharaoh refused. At last Pharaoh's heart was broken when his own son perished in plague sent by God. Pharaoh told Moses and the Israelites to leave Egypt. But soon Pharaoh hardened his heart again and sent his soldiers to bring the Israelites back to slavery.

Moses led the people out of Egypt into the desert along the seashore where they camped. When the people saw the Egyptian army coming they were terrified and cried out to the LORD and Moses, "Was it because there were no graves in Egypt that you brought us to the desert to die? Leave us alone! It would have been better for us to serve the Egyptians than to die in the desert!" Moses answered the people, "Do not be afraid. Stand firm and you will see the deliverance the LORD will bring you today. The LORD will fight for you."

Then the LORD said to Moses, "Raise your staff and stretch out your hand over the sea to divide the water so that the Israelites can pass through the sea on dry ground. For today I will harden the hearts of the Egyptians so they will attempt to follow. And I will gain glory through what happens to Pharaoh and all his army."

Then Moses obeyed God and stretched out his hand over the sea. All that night God pushed the sea back with strong wind and turned the seabed into dry ground. The waters were divided and the Israelites went through on dry ground, with a wall of water on their right and on their left.

The Egyptians pursued them but God made the wheels come off their chariots and confused the army. The Egyptians said, "Let's get away from the Israelites! Their God the LORD is fighting for them against Egypt."

Then the God said to Moses, "Stretch out your hand over the sea so that the waters may flow back over the Egyptians, their chariots and horsemen."

Moses obeyed God and stretched out his hand over the sea which returned to its place. The Egyptians were overcome by the returning waters that flowed over their chariots and horsemen. The entire army of Pharaoh perished.

But the Israelites had passed through the sea on dry ground as God promised. That day God saved Israel from the hands of the Egyptians. When the Israelites saw the great power God displayed against the Egyptians, the people feared the LORD God and put their trust in him and in Moses his servant.

Then Moses and the Israelites sang a song to God:

*I will sing to the Lord, for he is highly exalted. The horse and rider he has hurled into the sea...Who among the gods is like you, O Lord? Who is like you—majestic in holiness, awesome in glory, working wonders* (Exodus 15:1, 11).

# WATER STORIES

## 7. Abundant Water
## From the Rock

*Bible Reference:* Exodus 15:22-25, 27; 17:1-6

After many years had passed the descendants of Abraham had gone to live in the land of Egypt. At first the Egyptians treated Abraham's people well. God was blessing the descendants of Abraham for they had now become very great in number just as God had promised. But a time came when the Egyptians became fearful of the people who were now called Israelites. So the Egyptians made slaves of them, putting the Israelites to work making bricks with mud and straw. Their Egyptian taskmasters oppressed the Israelites greatly so they suffered.

In time God raised up a deliverer named Moses who was able to free the Israelites from the oppression of the Egyptians and lead the Israelites out of Egypt back toward the land of Abraham. After leaving Egypt the Israelites traveled three days in the desert without finding any water. When the Israelites finally came to water it was bitter and they could not drink it. The people grumbled against their leader Moses saying, "What are we to drink?"

Moses cried out to God on behalf of the people. Then God showed Moses a piece of wood. Moses took the piece of wood and threw it into the bitter water, and the water became sweet. Next God led the Israelites to a place where there were twelve springs of water and seventy palm trees. There was abundant water for all.

Their journey continued as God led them. Next the Israelites came to another place, but there was no water for the people to drink. So again the people quarreled with their leader Moses saying, "Give us water to drink." Again Moses cried out to God asking what to do. God said to

Moses, "Walk on ahead of the people. Take some of the elders of Israel with you, and take your staff in your hand. I will stand there before you by the rock at Horeb. Strike the rock and water will come out of it for the people to drink." So Moses did this in the sight of the elders as witnesses. Abundant water flowed freely for all.

Later one of Israel's prophets recalled the time in the desert when God provided water for the people. He said, *"He split the rocks in the desert and gave them water as abundant as the seas; he brought streams out of a rocky crag and made water flow down like rivers"* (Psalm 78:15-16).

After the time when Jesus, the one come from God, had returned to heaven, a spokesman for God said to the people in his say, *"I do not want you to be ignorant of the fact, brothers, that our forefathers were all under the cloud and all passed through the sea....They all ate the same spiritual food and drank from the spiritual rock that accompanied them, and that rock was Christ"* (1 Corinthians 10:1, 3-4).

God was able to provide abundant water for the Israelites in the days of Moses, even by splitting a rock to do so. The people were able to drink to their contentment from the abundant waters. Our physical thirst is a great need, to go without water soon leads to death. But there is a greater need, a spiritual need, for to go without the water of life, that is salvation, also leads to death, a terrible death of the spirit in an eternity of anguish and thirst that is never quenched. The invitation says: *"Come! Whoever is thirsty, let him come; and whoever wishes, let him take the free gift of the water of life"* (Revelation 22:17).

# WATER STORIES

## 8. A Drink for the Sheep

*Bible Reference:* Genesis 1:1-2; Psalm 23; 104:6-8, 10-11; 42:1-2

The Bible story begins: "In the beginning God created the heavens and the earth. Now the earth was at that time formless and empty, darkness was over the face of the deep, and the Spirit of God was hovering over the waters." The psalmist continues the story:

*"You (God) covered it with the deep as with a garment; the waters stood above the mountains. But at your rebuke the waters fled, at the sound of your thunder they took to flight; they flowed over the mountains, they went down into the valleys, to the place you assigned for them...He makes springs pour into the ravines; it flows between the mountains. They give water to the beasts of the field; the wild donkeys quench their thirst..."* (Psalm 104:6-8, 10-11).

In another place the psalmist writes:

*"As the deer pants for streams of water, so my soul pants for you, O God. My soul thirsts for God, for the living God"* (Psalm 42:1-2).

In another psalm, often called the Shepherd Psalm there is a poem like a story. It is like the words of a sheep speaking of his shepherd:

*"The LORD is my shepherd, I shall lack nothing. He makes me to lie down in green pastures, he leads me beside quiet waters. He restores my soul. He guides me in paths of righteousness for his name's sake. Even though I walk through the valley of the shadow of death, I will fear no evil, for you are with me, your rod and your staff, they*

35

*comfort me. You prepare a table before me in the presence of my enemies. You anoint my head with oil; my cup overflows. Surely goodness and love will follow me all the days of my life, and I will dwell in the house of the Lord forever."* (Psalm 23:1-6).

This is the story of one's life that trusts in God as his Shepherd. It is said that sheep will not drink from disturbed water. One of the jobs of the shepherd is to provide a quiet place where the water is undisturbed for the sheep to drink. And the psalmist has reminded us that it is God who provides that water from his abundant supply.

God has provided water for you to drink to meet the needs in this life. And God has provided a quiet pool for you to drink from to quench the thirst of your soul. Things happen to us to make us thirsty for this living water.

———

Here is a story from my grandfather who had a horse that he used to plow his fields each spring at planting time. The field was some distance from the barn where the horse was kept. And there was no water in the field, but there was water at the barn. Sometime the horse was not thirsty and so would not drink, though my grandfather knew the day would be hot and the horse would need water. So when my grandfather fed the horse he would put some salt in the food so the horse would soon become thirsty after eating. Then my grandfather would lead the horse to the water and the horse would drink deeply until his thirst was quenched. This reminds us things happen to us in our lives like that salt to make us thirsty so we will want to drink. But we must drink while the water is available and not when we want to. God has provided the water. Are you thirsty?

———

*"As the deer pants for streams of water, so my soul pants for you, O God. My soul thirsts for God, for the living God"* (Psalm 42:1-2).

36

# WATER STORIES

## 9. Water Too Precious To Drink

*Bible Reference:* 1 Samuel 8:5-6, 22; 10:1; 13:13-14; 16:5-13; 18:1-14; 22:1-2; 2 Samuel 23:8, 11,13-17

After many years had passed in the days of a prophet named Samuel the Israelites asked for a king, saying they wanted to be like all the other nations who had a king. God granted their wish and sent to Samuel a young man named Saul whom Samuel anointed as the first king of Israel. In the beginning Saul was a good king and obeyed all that God told him to do. But a time came when he began to do things his own way, that is, to be disobedient to what God asked him to do. So God told him the kingdom was going to be taken from him and given to another, a man after God's own heart.

So the prophet Samuel was sent to the home of a man with eight sons. Seven of the sons came to stand before Samuel who was thinking, "Surely this is the one." But each time God had said, "No, not that one. For man looks on the outward appearance, but God looks on the heart." When the last and youngest son was sent for, and came to stand before the prophet, God said, "He is the one. Arise and anoint him." So David was anointed as the new king. But David was still quite young and it would be many years yet before his enemies were defeated and he came to rule the people in peace.

During those early days David moved about with a band of his bodyguards, men who had come to join him and who were very brave and devoted to David. Those most brave were called his "mighty men." One had raised his spear against eight hundred of the enemy. Another took his stand in the middle of a field of lentils and, even when his own troops had fled away, he stood and defended the field until

37

a great victory was won. Such were the exploits of David's mighty men.

During the harvest time Philistines from a neighboring country had invaded the land and a garrison of them was camped near David's home in the town of Bethlehem. David and his men were in a stronghold, a cave above the valley were the enemy were camped. David had longed for water and happened to say, "Oh, that someone would get me a drink of water from the well near the gate of Bethlehem!"

Three of David's mighty men heard his request so they went and broke through the enemy lines and drew water from the well that is near the gate of Bethlehem. And they carried it back to David and presented it to him. But David refused to drink it; instead he poured it out before God and said, "Far be it from me, O God, to drink this! Is this not the blood of the men who went at the risk of their lives?" And so David would not drink the water.

The prophet Isaiah sang:

*"Surely God is my salvation; I will trust and not be afraid. The LORD, the LORD, is my strength and my song; he has become my salvation. With joy you will draw water from the wells of salvation....Give thanks to the LORD, call on his name; make known among the nations what he has done, and proclaim that his name is exalted"* (Isaiah 12:2-3).

And again the prophet said:

*"Come, all you who are thirsty, come to the waters ...Seek the LORD while he may be found; call on him while he is near. Let the wicked forsake his way and the evil man his thoughts. Let him turn to the LORD, and he will have mercy on him, and to our God, for he will have mercy on him, and to our God, for he will freely pardon"* (Isaiah 55:1a, 6-7).

The prophet Zechariah spoke of a coming day when abundant water would be available for cleansing from sin:

*"On that day a fountain will be opened to the house of David and the inhabitants of Jerusalem to cleanse them from sin and impurity"* (Zechariah 13:1).

The most precious water of all is the living water of salvation. It is abundant because the source of living water, Jesus, poured out his life for your sins. It is yours for cleansing from sin and to drink of its salvation.

———

*For we will surely die and become like water spilled on the ground, which cannot be gathered up again. Yet God does not take away a life; but He devises means, so that His banished ones are not expelled from Him* (2 Samuel 14:14).

# WATER STORIES

## 10. Only the True God
## Can Send Rain

*Bible Reference:* 1 Kings 16:30-33; 17:1; 18:1-2, 16-46

There was a king in the land of Israel who did more evil in the eyes of God than any king before him. Ahab not only considered it trivial to commit the sins of those before him who set up golden idols to worship, but he also married the daughter of a foreign king who brought into Ahab's kingdom her false religion of Baal worship and the fertility goddess. Baal was a foreign god who was worshiped as the god of storms and rain. It was supposed that he sent rain so that crops would grow and the cattle would be fat and fertile. The people in Ahab's kingdom were being led into sin by Ahab and his wife and her false prophets of Baal.

So God sent judgment upon the land of Israel because of their sin. The prophet Elijah said, "As the LORD, the God of Israel lives, whom I serve, there will be neither dew nor rain in the next few years except at my word." So there began a drought that was to last for three and a half years. Soon the crops began to fail and there was a severe famine, the grass died and the animals suffered, too. Even the king was out looking for grass to feed his horses.

Then the word of the LORD came to the prophet Elijah saying, "Go present yourself to King Ahab, and I will send rain upon the land." So Elijah went to present himself to Ahab.

When King Ahab saw Elijah he said to Elijah, "Is that you, you troubler of Israel?"

"I have not made trouble for Israel," Elijah replied. "But you have abandoned the LORD's commands and have followed the false god Baal. Now summon all the people of Israel to

41

meet me on the mountain. And bring the prophets of Baal and the prophets of the fertility goddess, too, who eat at the queen's table. So Ahab sent word throughout Israel. On the appointed day all the people assembled on the mountain.

Elijah went before the people and said, "How long will you waver between two opinions? If the LORD is God, follow him; but if Baal is God, follow him." But the people said nothing. Then Elijah spoke again, "I am the LORD's prophet, Baal has many prophets. Get two animals for our sacrifices. Let the prophets of Baal choose one for themselves and prepare it on their altar, but set no fire to it. Then have them call on the name of your god Baal. And I will call on the name of the LORD. The god who answers by fire—he is the true God."

Then all the people said, "What you say is good."

When the prophets of Baal had chosen their animal and prepared their altar with wood and the pieces of the animal, they began to call on the name of their god from morning till midday. "O Baal, answer us!" they shouted. But there was no reply, no one answered. They began to dance around the altar they had made. At midday Elijah began to taunt them. "Shout louder!" Elijah said. "Surely Baal is a god! Perhaps he is in deep thought, or busy, or traveling. Maybe he is sleeping and must be awakened." So the prophets shouted even louder and began to cut themselves with knives until blood flowed as was their custom. But there was no response; no one answered; no one paid attention.

Then Elijah said to all the people, "Come here to me." The people came to him, and Elijah repaired the altar of the LORD that lay in ruins. Taking twelve large stones he built an altar and then dug a trench about it large enough to hold a considerable amount of water. Elijah placed the wood on the altar and the pieces of the animal for the sacrifice.

Again Elijah said to the people, "Fill four large jars with water and pour it on the sacrifice and on the wood." When this was done he said, "Do it again!" And they did it again.

"Do it a third time!" he ordered and they did it a third time. Water ran down around the altar and even filled the trench.

At the time of the evening sacrifice Elijah stepped forward and prayed: "O LORD, God of Israel, let it be known today that you are the true God in Israel and I am your servant who has done all these things at your command. Answer me, O LORD, so these people will know that you alone are God, and that you are turning their hearts back again."

At Elijah's words the fire of the LORD fell from heaven and burned up the sacrifice, it burned up the wood and the stones and the soil, and also licked up the water in the trench.

When all the people saw this, they fell on their faces and cried out, "The LORD—he is God! The LORD—he is God!"

Elijah commanded that the false prophets be seized and put to death. He said to King Ahab, "Go, eat and drink, for there is the sound of a heavy rain." Elijah told his servant, "Go and look toward the sea." The servant went and looked but said to Elijah, "I looked but there is nothing there." Seven times Elijah told the servant to go back and look. The seventh time the servant reported, "A cloud as small as a man's hand is rising from the sea." So Elijah said, "Go and tell the king to hitch up his chariot and go down the mountain before the rain stops him." Meanwhile, the sky grew black with clouds, the wind began to blow, and a heavy rain fell upon the land. The drought was broken.

The Prophet Isaiah had this to say about God: *"This is what the LORD says...I am the first and I am the last; apart from me there is no God...For I will pour water on the thirsty land, and streams on the dry ground"* (Isaiah 44:6, 3).

The prophet Hosea had this to say: *"Let us acknowledge the Lord; let us press on to acknowledge him. As surely as the sun rises, he will appear; he will come to us like the winter rains, like the young rains that water the earth"* (Hosea 6:3).

*"Sow for yourselves righteousness, reap the fruit of unfailing love, and break up your unplowed ground; for it is*

*time to seek the Lord, until he comes and showers righteousness on you"* (Hosea 10:12).

But there was a warning for the people of that day if they turned from following the true God and obeying his commands. God warned: *"If you do not obey the LORD your God and do not carefully follow all his commands and decrees....The sky over your head will be bronze, the ground beneath you iron. The LORD will turn the rain of your country into dust and powder; it will come down from the skies until you are ruined"* (Deuteronomy 28:15a, 23-24).

———

*For thus says the LORD: "You shall not see wind, nor shall you see rain; yet that valley shall be filled with water, so that you, your cattle, and your animals may drink"* (2 Kings 3:17).

# WATER STORIES

## 11. The Man Made Clean
## In a Muddy River

*Bible Reference:* 2 Kings 5:1-19

Naaman was a commander of the army in the land of Aram. He was a great man in the sight of his king and highly regarded because of the victories God had given him. He was a valiant soldier, but he had leprosy.

One of the raiding parties down into the land of Israel had taken captive a young girl who served Naaman's wife. One day the girl said to her mistress, "If only my master would see the prophet who lives in Israel. He would cure him of his leprosy."

So Naaman went to his king and told him what the girl had said. The king encouraged Naaman to go to Israel to be cured. And the king said, "I will send a letter to the king of Israel and a large gift of gold, silver and clothing." The letter to the king of Israel read like this: "With this letter I am sending my servant Naaman to you so that you may cure him of his leprosy."

As soon as the king of Israel read the letter he began to tear his royal robes and cried out, "Am I God? Can I kill and bring back to life? Why does the king of Aram send someone to me to be cured of his leprosy? See, he is trying to pick a quarrel with me!"

When the prophet Elisha, the man of God, heard that the king had torn his robes, he sent him this message: "Why have you torn your robes? Have the foreign man come to me and he will know there is a prophet of God in Israel."

So Naaman went with his horses and chariots and stopped at the door of Elisha's house. Elisha sent a messenger out to say to Naaman, "Go, wash yourself seven times in the

45

Jordan River, and your flesh will be restored and you will be cleansed of your leprosy."

But Naaman went away angry and said, I thought the prophet would surely come out to me and stand and call on the name of the LORD his God, wave his hand over the leprosy and cure me. Are not the clear rivers of Damascus in my home country better than the muddy waters of Israel? Couldn't I wash in them and be healed? So Namaan turned and went off in a rage.

Naaman's servants went to him and said, "My father, if the prophet had told you to do some great thing, would you not have done it? How much more, then, when he tells you, 'Wash and be cleansed!'"

So Naaman went down to the Jordan River, as the man of God had told him, and dipped himself in the river seven times. His flesh was restored and became clean like that of a young boy.

Then Naaman and all his servants went back to the man of God. He stood before Elisha and said, "Now I know that there is no God in all the world except in Israel. Please accept now a gift from your servant."

But Elisha answered, "As surely as the LORD lives, whom I serve, I will not accept a thing." And even though Naaman urged him, Elisha refused. "Go in peace," Elisha said.

Before the earthly ministry of Jesus began there was a prophet named John who was filled with the Spirit of God from his birth. He was sent by God to prepare the way for the coming Messiah, the Promised Anointed One of God. John lived in the desert, dressed in rough clothing, eating wild foods. He began to preach that people must confess their sins, repent, and be baptized for the kingdom of God was near at hand. Many came to hear John and believed, confessing their sins and repenting, and were baptized by John in the Jordan River as a picture of washing away their sins (*Acts 22:16*). John said, "I baptize with water, but one is coming who is greater than I, and he will baptize with the Holy Spirit."

46

*"Wash yourselves, make yourselves clean; put away the evil of your doings from before My eyes. Cease to do evil, Learn to do good; seek justice, rebuke the oppressor; defend the fatherless, plead for the widow"* (Isaiah 1:16-17).

# WATER STORIES

## 12. Change of Heart
## At the Bottom of the Sea

*Bible Reference:* Jonah 1-4; Proverbs 15:3

A certain people living in a city called Nineveh were very sinful in the eyes of the LORD whose eyes are everywhere keeping watch on the wicked and the good. So the word of the LORD came to a prophet named Jonah saying: "Go to the great city of Nineveh and preach against it, because its wickedness has come up before me."

But Jonah ran away from the LORD and instead headed for the seaport where he paid the fare and boarded a ship.

While Jonah was fleeing from the LORD, the LORD sent a great wind on the sea and such a violent storm arose that the ship threatened to break up. All the sailors were afraid and each began to cry out to his own god to save him from the storm. The sailors even threw all the cargo into the sea to lighten the ship. Jonah had gone down inside the ship where he lay down and was fast asleep.

The ship's captain awakened Jonah saying, "How can you sleep? Get up and call on your god! Maybe he will take notice of us and we will not perish."

The sailors cast lots to see who was responsible for the storm. The lot fell on Jonah who confessed, "I am running away from my God. I worship the LORD, the God of heaven, who made the sea and the land." Then Jonah added, "If you pick me up and throw me into the sea it will become calm. I know it is my fault this great storm has come upon you."

The sailors did their best to save the ship but the storm increased its fury. They cried to the LORD, "Do not hold us accountable for killing this man." Then the sailors took

49

Jonah and threw him overboard and the raging sea became calm.

The LORD had prepared a great fish to swallow Jonah, and Jonah was inside the fish three days and three nights.

From inside the fish Jonah prayed to the LORD his God. He said:

"In my distress I called on the LORD, and he answered me....I called for help and you listened to my cry. You hurled me into the deep, into the very heart of the sea, and the currents swirled about me, all your waves swept over me.... seaweed was wrapped around my head.... But you brought my life up from the pit. When my life was ebbing away, I remembered you, LORD, and my prayer rose to you in your holy temple. For those who cling to worthless idols forfeit the grace that could be theirs. With a song of thanksgiving I will sacrifice to you and what I have vowed I will make good. Salvation comes from the LORD."

The LORD commanded the fish and it spit Jonah out onto dry land. Then the word of the LORD came to Jonah a second time saying: "Go to that great city of Nineveh and proclaim to it the message I give you."

Jonah obeyed the word of the LORD and went to Nineveh. Now Nineveh was a very large city so it took three days for Jonah to go all through it proclaiming the LORD's message: "Forty more days and Nineveh will be destroyed."

When the people of Nineveh heard the message they believed God. So they declared a fast and all of them from the greatest to the least put on sackcloth as a sign of their repentance. Even the king arose from his throne, removed his royal robes, covered himself with sackcloth and sat in the dust. The king issued a decree saying: "Do not let any man or beast, herd or flock, taste anything, do not let them eat or drink. Let all the animals be covered with sackcloth. Let everyone call urgently on God. Let them give up their evil ways and their violence. Perhaps God may relent and with compassion turn from his fierce anger so that we may not perish."

When God saw what the people did and how they turned from their evil ways, He did have compassion on the people of Nineveh and did not bring upon them the destruction He had promised.

Jonah was angry that God had spared the wicked people of Nineveh instead of destroying them. Jonah said that was why he ran away in the ship because he knew God would be gracious and compassionate, a God slow to anger and abounding in love.

The LORD said to Jonah, "Nineveh has more than a hundred and twenty thousand people who cannot tell their right hand from their left, and many cattle as well. Should I not be concerned about that great city?"

———

*"Then I acknowledged my sin to you and did not cover up my iniquity. I said, 'I will confess my transgressions to the LORD'— and you forgave the guilt of my sin. Selah*

*Therefore let everyone who is godly pray to you while you may be found; surely when the mighty waters rise, they will not reach him.*

*Many are the woes of the wicked, but the LORD's unfailing love surrounds the man who trusts in him"* (Psalm 32:5-6, 10).

# WATER STORIES

## 13. Streams in the Desert
## And Broken Cisterns

*Bible Reference:* Exodus 19:5-6; Deuteronomy 11:10-17; Joshua 24:19, 21, 24; Judges 2:10. 12, 16, 19; Isaiah 41:17-18; Jeremiah 2:13; 44:5-6, 16; Ezekiel 36:25-28

The prophet named Isaiah wrote: "The poor and the needy search for water, but there is none; their tongues are parched with thirst. But I the LORD will answer them; I the God of Israel, will not forsake them. I will make rivers flow on barren heights, and springs within the valleys. I will turn the desert into pools of water, and the parched ground into springs (Isaiah 41:17-18).

Another prophet brought a word of serious condemnation from God to the people in his day. He said, "My people have committed two sins: They have forsaken me, the spring of living water, and have .dug their own cisterns, broken cisterns that cannot hold water" (Jeremiah 2:13).

Long before God had called the man named Abraham and promised to give him many descendants, and through one of his descendants to bless all peoples. From Abraham and his family God raised up a people called the Israelites. He told them, "If you obey me fully and keep my covenant, then out of all nations you will be my treasured possession. Although the whole earth is mine, you will be for me a kingdom of priests and a holy nation" (Exodus 19:5-6).

Before God led the people into the land He promised them God said:

"The land you are entering to take over is not like the land of Egypt, from which you have come, where you planted your seed and irrigated it by foot as in a vegetable garden. But the land you are to take possession of is a land of mountains and valleys that drinks rain from heaven. It is a land the LORD your God cares for; the eyes of the LORD your God are continually on it from the beginning of the year to its end.

So, if you faithfully obey the commands I am giving you today—to love the LORD your God and serve him with all your heart and with all your soul—then I will send rain on your land in its season, both autumn and spring rains, so that you may gather in your grain, new wine and oil. I will provide grass in the fields for your cattle, and you will eat and be satisfied.

Be careful, or you will be enticed to turn away and worship other gods and bow down to them. Then the LORD's anger will burn against you, and he will shut the heavens so that it will not rain and the ground will yield no produce, and you will soon perish from the good land the LORD is giving you" (Deuteronomy 11:10-17).

Before their leader Joshua died he called the people to him and said, "You are not able to serve the LORD. He is a holy God, he is a jealous God. He will not forgive your rebellion and your sins. If you forsake the LORD and serve foreign gods, he will turn and bring disaster on you, after he has been good to you" (*Joshua 24:19-20*). But the people said, "No! We will serve the LORD our God and obey him" (*Joshua 24:24*).

After that generation died another generation grew up who neither knew the LORD nor what he had done for Israel. Then the Israelites did evil in the eyes of the LORD. They turned from the LORD and followed and worshiped various gods of the people around them. The LORD punished them and when the people repented and cried out to God, He sent a deliverer to save them from their enemies. But soon after the deliverer's lifetime, the people again fell into sin and prostituted themselves by serving other gods. This happened many times in the passing years. Until at last the kingdom had become very corrupt even after being warned many times by the prophets that God sent.

And so God had raised up the prophet Jeremiah and sent him to tell the people what was going to happen to them.

But the people did not listen or pay attention; they did not turn from their wickedness or stop burning incense to other gods. So God poured out not the promised rains if the people were faithful, but his fierce anger because of their stubbornness. Even after hearing Jeremiah's words of coming disaster the people said, "We will not listen to the message you have spoken to us in the name of the LORD. We will certainly do everything we said we would" (Jeremiah 44:16-17).

And so it was that God accused the people of forsaking Him, the spring of living water, and digging for themselves their own cisterns, broken cisterns that cannot hold water. And disaster fell on the people.

But God is a God of mercy and love. Another prophet speaking of the future days spoke these words from God, "I will sprinkle clean water on you, and you will be clean; I will cleanse you from all your impurities and from all your idols. I will give you a new heart and put a new spirit in you; I will remove your heart of stone and give you a heart of flesh. And I will put my Spirit in you and move you to follow my decrees and be careful to keep my laws. You will live in the land I gave your forefathers; you will be my people, and I will be your God" (Ezekiel 36:25-28).

The evangelist John wrote to people in his day, *"If we confess our sins, he is faithful and just and will forgive us our sins and purify us from all unrighteousness. The blood of Jesus, God's Son, purifies us from all sin"* (1 John 1:9, 7).

———

*"I will give them a new heart to know me, that I am the LORD. They will be my people, and I will be their God, for they will return to me with all their heart"* (Jeremiah 24:7).

# WATER STORIES

## 14. Repentance and Baptism

*Bible Reference:* Matthew 3:13-17; 28:19-20; Luke 3:4, 6, 9-10, 15-16, 18

The ancient prophets foretold the birth of the coming Messiah or Christ. The time came when Jesus was born of a virgin in Bethlehem just as the prophets said would happen. When he was about 30 years of age Jesus began his public ministry.

About the same time a prophet named John the Baptist (or one who baptizes) came preaching a baptism of repentance for the forgiveness of sins. He was a voice in the desert calling, "Prepare the way for the Lord, make straight paths for him....And all mankind will see God's salvation."

John spoke to the crowds coming out to be baptized. He called for the people to produce fruit (live a life) in keeping with repentance. John said the axe is already at the root of the trees, and every tree that does not produce good fruit will be cut down and thrown into the fire."

"What should we do?" the people asked John.

John replied they must live righteous lives that were pleasing to God. The people were wondering if John might be the Christ who was to come. But John answered, "I baptize you with water for repentance. But one more powerful than I will come. I am not worthy to untie the laces of his sandals. He will baptize you with the Holy Spirit and with fire." And with many other words John warned the people and preached the good news to them.

The people were confessing their sins and John baptized them. While all the people were being baptized in the river, John saw Jesus coming toward him. John declared, "Look, the Lamb of God, who takes away the sin of the world."

Then John said to Jesus, "I need to be baptized by you, and do you come to me?"

Jesus replied, "Let it be so now; it is proper for us to do this to fulfill righteousness." So John baptized Jesus there in the river. As Jesus went up out of the water, heaven was opened and John saw the Spirit of God descending on Jesus like a dove. And a voice from heaven said, "This is my Son, whom I love. With him I am well pleased.

Later Jesus taught his disciples that they were to go and make disciples of all the nations, and to baptize the people in the name of God the Father, the Son and the Holy Spirit. And the disciples were to teach the people all things that Jesus commanded them. Jesus promised to be with his followers even to the end of the world.

———

"....having been buried with him (Christ) in baptism and raised with him through your faith in the power of God, who raised him (Christ) from the dead." (Colossians 2:12).

# WATER STORIES

## 15. Blessed Are Those Who Hunger And Thirst for Righteousness

*Bible Reference:* Psalm 42:2; 63:1; 143:6; Matthew 5:6

Jesus had been going throughout the region of Galilee teaching in the worship halls, preaching the good news of the kingdom of God, and healing every disease and sickness among the people. News about Jesus had spread all over that region and people brought to him all who were ill with various diseases, those suffering severe pain, the demon-possessed, the epileptics and those paralyzed, and Jesus healed them all. Large crowds followed Jesus. When Jesus saw the crowds, he went up on the mountainside and sat down. Jesus' disciples came to him and he began to teach them, saying:

*"Blessed are the poor in spirit, for theirs is the kingdom of heaven.*

*Blessed are those who mourn, for they will be comforted.*

*Blessed are the meek for they will inherit the earth.*

*Blessed are those who hunger and thirst for righteousness, for they will be filled.*

*Blessed are the merciful, for they will be shown mercy.*

*Blessed are the pure in heart, for they will see God.*

*Blessed are the peacemakers, for they will be called sons of God.*

*Blessed are those who are persecuted because of righteousness, for theirs is the kingdom of God"* (Matthew 5:3-8).

Jesus taught that not all desires were harmful, in fact, some were to be encouraged. Two of the desires to be satisfied were that of spiritual hunger and thirst. Long before the psalmist cried out: "My soul thirsts for God, for the living God...O God, you are my God, earnestly I seek you, my

59

soul thirsts for you...in a dry and weary land where there is no water...I spread out my hands to you; my soul thirsts for you like a parched land" (Psalm 63:1).

For in those days the people longed for God's presence with them like a thirsty man longs for a drink of water. For the faithful the prophet Isaiah said, "The LORD will guide you always; he will satisfy your needs in a sun-scorched land and will strengthen your frame. You will be like a well-watered garden, like a spring whose waters never fail" (Isaiah 58:11).

God is a merciful God for Jesus reminded the people, "Your Father in heaven causes his sun to rise on the evil and on the good, and sends rain on the righteous and the unrighteous." But for those who persist in their sin there is a time of drought coming. Long ago a prophet named Amos warned the people of his day, "'The days are coming,' declares the Sovereign Lord, 'when I will send a famine through the land—not a famine of food or a thirst for water, but a famine of hearing the words of the LORD. Men will stagger from sea to sea and wander from north to east, searching for the word of the LORD, but they will not find it" (Amos 8:11-12).

———

But for those who seek the Lord, who turn from their sin, "Never again will they hunger, never again will they thirst" (Revelation 7:16).

For he satisfies the thirsty and fills the hungry with good things (Psalm 107:9).

# WATER STORIES

## 16. A Drink of Living Water

*Bible Reference:* 2 Kings 17:24-25, 27, 29, 33-34; John 4:4-30, 39-42; 7:37-38

A long time before this story the people who lived in the old Kingdom of Israel had fallen into grievous sin against the LORD their God. He warned them again and again but the people did not listen or repent. So God allowed a foreign nation to come and take away captives and bring other peoples to live in their land. These peoples brought their own gods to worship and also tried to worship the LORD as well. Later on the people were considered low caste because of their mixed blood and their idolatry. The Jewish people of Jesus' day did not like to pass through their province of Samaria or have anything to do with them.

One day Jesus with his disciples journeyed through Samaria. At mid-day they came to a well that had been dug in the days of Jacob, the grandson of Abraham. Jesus sat down to rest. Soon a Samaritan woman came with her rope and water jar to draw water. When she came near Jesus said to her, "Will you give me a drink?" The woman was surprised and said to Jesus, "You are a Jew and I am a Samaritan woman. How can you ask me for a drink?" The woman knew that Jews had nothing to do with Samaritans.

Jesus answered her, "If you knew the gift of God and who it is that asks you for a drink, you would have instead asked him, and he would have given you living water."

"Sir," the woman said, "you have nothing which to draw water, and the well is deep. Where can you get this living water? Are you greater than our ancestor Jacob who gave us the well and drank from it himself, as did his sons and his flocks and herds?"

Jesus answered, "Everyone who drinks this water will be thirsty again. But whoever drinks the water I give him will never thirst. Indeed, the water I give him will become in him a spring of water, bubbling up to eternal life."

The woman was very interested in the words of Jesus and said, "Sir, give me this water so that I won't get thirsty and have to keep coming to this well to draw water."

Jesus told her, "Go call your husband and come back."

"I have no husband," she replied.

Then Jesus said, "You are right when you say you have no husband. The fact is, you have had five husbands, and the man you now live with is not your husband. What you said is quite true."

To justify herself the woman said, "Sir, I can see that you are a prophet. Our ancestors worshiped on this mountain, but you Jews claim that the only place we must worship is in Jerusalem."

Jesus declared, "Believe me, woman, a time is coming when you will worship God neither on this mountain nor in Jerusalem. You Samaritans worship what you do not know. We worship what we do know, for salvation is from the Jews. A time is coming when true worshipers will worship God in spirit and in truth, for they are the kind of worshipers God seeks. God is a spirit, and his worshipers must worship him in spirit and in truth."

The woman said, "I know the Messiah (the Promised Anointed One) is coming. When he comes he will explain everything to us."

Then Jesus declared, "I who speak to you am the Messiah."

The woman left her water jar and went back to town and said to the people, "Come, see a man who told me everything I ever did. Could he be the Messiah, the Christ?"

The people came out of the town and invited Jesus to stay with them, and Jesus stayed two days. Many of the Samaritans from that town believed in Jesus because of the woman's testimony. Because of Jesus' words many more became believers. The people said to the woman, "We no longer believe just because of what you said; now we have heard for ourselves, and we know that this Jesus really is the Savior of the world."

**Note**: It is said that the Jewish people of that day preferred to drink water that came from a spring, that was bubbling and flowing, that was *alive*. Jacob's well is still there today. It is 105 feet deep and at the bottom an archaeologist discovered a flowing spring of water—*alive* or *living* water. But the living water Jesus offered was *better water*. After drinking water from the well one soon became thirsty again.

The water Jesus offered was *living water* that satisfied and that bubbled up inside a person to eternal life. John's Gospel says, "Whoever believes in Jesus, as the Scripture has said, streams of living water will flow from within." By this he meant the Spirit, whom those who believed were later to receive. (*John 7:38-39*) "Let them give thanks to the LORD for his unfailing love...for he satisfies the thirsty" (Psalm 107:8a, 9a).

———

*Jesus answered, "Everyone who drinks this water will be thirsty again, but whoever drinks the water I give him will never thirst. Indeed, the water I give him will become in him a spring of water welling up to eternal life"* (John 4:13-14).

# WATER STORIES

## 17. Jesus Calmed the Stormy Sea

*Bible Reference:* Mark 4:33-41; Matthew 14:22-36

Jesus taught the people as much as they could understand using parables. That day when evening came, Jesus said to his disciples, "Let us go over to the other of the lake." So Jesus left the crowd behind and the disciples took Jesus along in their boat. A terrible storm came up and the waves began to break over into the boat so that it was nearly sinking.

Jesus was asleep in the back of the boat, resting on a cushion. His disciples were afraid and woke Jesus saying, "Teacher, don't you care if we drown?"

Jesus got up, rebuked the wind and the waves saying, "Quiet! Be still!" Then the wind died down and the water was completely calm.

Jesus said to his disciples, "Why are you so afraid? Do you have no faith?"

The disciples were terrified and asked each other, "Who is this? Even the wind and the waves obey him!"

At another time Jesus had fed more than 5,000 people with only five loaves of bread and two fish. Immediately afterward Jesus made his disciples get into a boat and go ahead of him to the other side of the lake while Jesus sent the crowd away. After the crowd departed Jesus went up into the hills by himself to pray.

When evening came, Jesus was there alone. The boat was already a considerable distance from land. The wind was strong and the boat was buffeted by the high waves. During the night Jesus came to the disciples walking on the lake.

When the disciples saw Jesus walking on the lake, they were terrified. "It's a ghost!" they cried out in fear.

But Jesus immediately said to the disciples, "Take courage! It is I. Don't be afraid."

"Lord, if it's you, tell me to come to you on the water," the disciple named Peter said.

Jesus said, "Come!"

Then Peter got down out of the boat and walked on the water to Jesus. But when Peter saw the wind, he was afraid and began to sink into the water. He cried out, "Lord, save me!"

Immediately Jesus reached out his hand and caught Peter. "You of little faith," Jesus said. "Why did you doubt?"

After they climbed into the boat, the wind died down. The disciples in the boat worshiped Jesus saying, "Truly you are the Son of God."

When they had crossed over to the other side, the people recognized Jesus and sent word to others in the surrounding countryside. People brought all their sick to Jesus. And all who touched Jesus were healed.

*"Then Jesus came to them and said, "All authority in heaven and on earth has been given to me."* (Matthew 18:19).

# WATER STORIES

## 18. A Drink of Water
## In Jesus' Name

*Bible Reference:* Proverbs 25:21; 2 Kings 6:8-23; Matthew 5:43-46; 10:42; 25:34-40

A proverb says: "If your enemy is hungry, give him food to eat; if he is thirsty, give him water to drink" *(Proverbs 25:21).*

During the days of the prophets the king of Aram was at war with the king of Israel. But each time the king of Aram would plan to set his camp in a certain place the king of Israel would already know about it. Time and again the prophet Elisha would warn the king of Israel. This enraged the king of Aram who summoned his officers and demanded, "Will you tell me which one of you is on the side of the king of Israel, telling him where we will be?"

"None of us, my king," said one of the officers, "it is that prophet Elisha who is in Israel who tells the king of Israel even the very words you speak in your bedroom!"

"Go, find out where he is," the king ordered, "so I can capture him." After the officers returned and said where Elisha was staying, the king sent horses and chariots and a strong force to surround the city by night.

When the servant of Elisha arose and went out early the next morning, an army with horses and chariots surrounded the city. "Oh, my lord," the servant cried to Elisha, "what shall we do?"

"Don't be afraid," the prophet answered. "Those who are with us are more than those who are with them."

And then Elisha prayed, "O LORD, open my servant's eyes so he may see." Then the LORD opened the servant's eyes, and he looked and saw the hills full of horses and chariots of fire all around Elisha.

As the enemy came toward him, Elisha prayed to the LORD, "Strike these people with blindness." So the LORD struck the enemy with blindness, as Elisha had asked.

Elisha then told the enemy, "This is not the road, and this is not the city. Follow me, and I will lead you to the man you are looking for." And so Elisha led the enemy soldiers to the city of Samaria where the king of Israel lived. After they entered the city, Elisha said, "LORD, open the eyes of these men so they can see." Then the LORD opened their eyes and they looked, and saw they were inside the city of Samaria!

When the king of Israel saw the enemy troops, he asked Elisha, "Shall I kill them, my father? Shall I kill them?"

"Do not kill them," Elisha answered. "Would you kill men you have captured with your own sword or bow? Set food and water before them so they may eat and drink and go back to their master." So the king prepared a great feast for the men, and after they had finished eating and drinking, he sent them away, and they returned to their own king.

Jesus taught his followers about those who were their enemies. He said, "You have heard it was said, "Love your neighbor and hate your enemy. But I tell you: Love your enemies and pray for those who persecute you, that you may be sons of your Father in heaven. For God causes his sun to rise on the evil and the good, and sends rain on the righteous and the unrighteous. If you love those who love you, what reward will you get?"

One day an expert in religious law tested Jesus by asking him, "Teacher, what must I do to inherit eternal life?" Jesus asked the man what was written in the law. He replied, "Love the LORD your God with all your heart and with all your soul and with all your strength and with all your mind; and love your neighbor as yourself."

"You have answered correctly," Jesus replied. "Do this and you will live."

But the man wanted to justify himself, so he asked Jesus, "And who is my neighbor?"

In reply Jesus said, "A man was going down from Jerusalem to Jericho, when he fell into the hands of robbers. They stripped him of his clothes, beat him and went away, leaving him half dead. A religious leader happened to be going down the same road, and when he saw the man, he passed by on the other side. Again a religious worker came to the place and saw the man; and he too passed by on the other side. Then along came a Samaritan, one of those people despised by the Jewish people. As he came to where the man lay, the Samaritan took pity on him. The Samaritan went to him and bandaged his wounds, pouring on medicine. Then the Samaritan put the man on his donkey and took the man to an inn and cared for him. The next day the Samaritan took out two silver coins and gave them to the innkeeper. 'Look after the wounded man,' the Samaritan said, 'and when I return, I will reimburse you for any extra expense you may have.'

Which of these three men do you think was a neighbor to the man who fell into the hands of robbers?" Jesus asked. The expert in the law said, "The one who had mercy on the man." So Jesus told him, "Go, and do likewise."

Another time when Jesus was speaking of doing good works he said, "If anyone gives a cup of cold water to one of these little ones because he is my disciple, I tell you the truth, he will certainly not lose his reward" (*Matthew 10:42*).

Teaching about righteousness Jesus said, "The King will say to those on his right, 'Come, you who are blessed by my Father; take your inheritance, a kingdom prepared for you since the creation of the world. For I was hungry and you gave me something to eat, I was thirsty and you gave me something to drink, I was a stranger and you invited me in, I needed clothes and you clothed me, I was sick and you looked after me, I was in prison and you came to visit me.'

Then the righteous will answer him, 'Lord, when did we see you hungry and feed you, or thirsty and give you something to drink? When did we see you a stranger and invite you in, or needing clothes and clothe you? When did we see you sick or in prison and go to visit you?

The King will reply, 'I tell you the truth, whatever you did for the least of these brothers of mine, you did for me'" (*Matthew 25:34-40*).

Has anyone given you a drink of cold water?

Have you given anyone a drink of cold water, even those who are your enemies? It is the least you can do for them. The King would be pleased.

———

*They feast on the abundance of your house; you give them drink from your river of delights.*
*For with you is the fountain of life; in your light we see light.*
*Continue your love to those who know you, your righteousness to the upright in heart* (Psalm 36:8-10).

# WATER STORIES

## 19. The Man Born Blind
## Who Washed and Could See

*Bible References*: John 9:1-41; 2 Corinthians 4:4; Revelation 3:17-18

One day as Jesus walked along with his disciples, he saw a man blind from his birth. Jesus' disciples asked him, "Teacher, who sinned, this man or his parents that he was born blind?"

"Neither this man nor his parents sinned," said Jesus, "but this happened so that the work of God might be displayed in his life. For while I am in the world, I am the light of the world."

Having said these words, Jesus spit on the ground, made some mud with his saliva, and put it on the man's eyes. "Go," he told the man, "wash in the Pool of Siloam." So the man went, and washed, and came home seeing.

His neighbors and those who had formerly seen him begging asked, "Isn't this the same man who used to sit and beg? Some claimed that he was. Others said, "No, he only looks like him."

But the man born blind insisted, "I am the man."

"Then how were your eyes opened?" they demanded.

He replied, "The man they call Jesus made some mud and put it on my eyes. He told me to go to Siloam Pool and wash. So I went and washed, and then I could see."

"Where is this man?" they asked him.

"I don't know," he said.

So the people brought the man to the Pharisees. It happened that the day on which Jesus had made the mud and opened the man's eyes was a Sabbath, a day on which their law prohibited any work. So the Pharisees asked the man how it was that he had received his sight.

"He put mud on my eyes," the man explained, "and I washed, and now I see."

Some of the Pharisees were saying, "This man Jesus is not from God. He does not keep the Sabbath law. He is a sinner." But others were asking, "How can a sinner do such miraculous signs?" So they were divided in their opinions. Finally they turned to the blind man again, "What have you to say about Jesus? It was your eyes he opened." The man replied, "He is a prophet."

The leaders still did not believe that the man had been blind and had received his sight. So the leaders sent for the man's parents. "Is this your son?" they asked. "Is this the one you say was born blind? How is it that he can see?"

"We know he is our son," the parents answered, "and we know he was born blind. But how he can see now, or who opened his eyes, we don't know. Ask him. He is of age; he will speak for himself." His parents said this because they were afraid of the religious leaders for they had already decided that anyone who acknowledged that Jesus was the Christ would be put out of the worship hall.

So a second time the religious leaders summoned the man and said, "Give glory to God. We know this man Jesus is a sinner!"

"Whether he is a sinner or not, I don't know," the man answered. "One thing I do know. I was born blind but now I see!"

Then the leaders asked him again, "What did he do to you? How did he open your eyes?" But the man said, "I have told you already but you didn't listen. Why do you want to hear it again?" Then the religious leaders hurled insults at the man because he was saying, "God does not listen to sinners. He listens to the godly man who does his will. Nobody has ever heard of opening the eyes of a man born blind. If this man were not from God, he could do nothing."

To this reply the religious leaders said, "How dare you to lecture us! You were steeped in sin at your birth." And the leaders threw the man out.

Jesus heard what had happened so he found the man and asked, "Do you believe in the Son of Man?" "Who is he, sir?" the man asked. "Tell me so that I may believe in him."

Jesus said, "You have seen him; in fact, he is the one speaking with you now." Then the man said, "Lord, I believe," and the man worshiped Jesus.

Jesus added, "For judgment I have come into this world, so that the blind will see and those who see will become blind."

Some Pharisees who were standing there heard Jesus say these words and asked, "What! Are we blind too?"

Jesus said, "If you were blind, you would not be guilty of sin; but now that you claim you can see, your guilt remains."

In a prophecy to group of believers Jesus spoke these words: "You say, 'I am rich; I have acquired wealth and do not need a thing. But you do not realize that you are wretched, pitiful, poor, blind and naked. I counsel you to buy from me gold refined in the fire, white clothes to wear to cover your shameful nakedness, and salve to put on your eyes, so you can see" (*Revelation 3:17-18*). The Evangelist Paul said, "It is the god of this age, that is, Satan, who has blinded the eyes of unbelievers, so they cannot see the light of the gospel of the glory of Christ" (*2 Corinthians 4:4*).

How are your eyes? Do you need to wash in the fountain and have your vision restored? Can you see Jesus?

———

*Open my eyes, that I may see wondrous things from Your law* (Psalm 119:18).

# WATER STORIES

## 20. The Man Who Could
## Not Get Into the Water

*Bible Reference:* John 5:1-15; Romans 5:8; Ephesians 2:4, 8-9

It was one of the feast times of the Jews when Jesus went up to Jerusalem. In the city near the Sheep Gate there was a pool fed by an intermittent spring of mineral water that in the language of that day was called Bethesda which means *house of mercy or house of compassion*. Instead it was a place of misery for a great number of disabled people gathered there and were lying about—the blind, the lame, and the paralyzed—by the pool that was surrounded by five covered porches. One man there had been an invalid without any strength for thirty-eight years.

When Jesus saw this man lying there and learned that he had been in this weak condition for a long time, Jesus pitied him and so asked the man, "Do you want to get well?"

"Sir," the invalid replied, "It's hopeless. I have no one to quickly put me into the pool whenever the water is stirred. While I am trying to get into the water, someone else goes down ahead of me." For the people believed that when the waters bubbled it was an angel coming down from time to time and disturbing the waters, energizing them so that whoever stepped in first would be healed.

Then Jesus said to the man, "Get up! Pick up your bed and walk." At once the man was cured; he picked up his bed and walked.

The day on which this took place was a Sabbath, the day when the law required that no work be done. So the religious leaders who had no joy in their stony hearts over the man's healing said to the man who had been healed, "It is the Sabbath, the law forbids you to carry your bed."

But the man replied, "The man who made me well said to me, 'Pick up your bed and walk'."

So the leaders asked him, "Who is this fellow who told you to pick up your bed and walk?"

The man who had been healed by the pool had no idea who it was, for Jesus had slipped away into the crowd of people in that place.

Later Jesus found the man at the temple and said to him, "See, you are well again. Stop sinning or something worse may happen to you."

The man went on his way and told the religious leaders that it was Jesus who had made him well.

The Bible says "While we were still sinners Christ died for us" (*Romans 5:8*). And "God, who is rich in mercy, made us alive with Christ even when we were dead in transgressions—it is by God's grace we have been saved, through our faith, not by any works that we do, lest we should boast" (*Ephesians 2:4b-9*).

How long have you been waiting to get into the water of God's mercy and be healed? Do you want to get well?

———

*I said, "LORD, be merciful to me; heal my soul, for I have sinned against You"* (Psalm 41:4).

# WATER STORIES

## 21. A Thirsty Man
## Who Begged for Water

*Bible Reference:* Luke 12:13-21; 16:19-31

These stories are not about the danger of riches, but of forgetting God and not taking seriously his words spoken through the prophets. Both are stories that Jesus told the people gathered around him.

Someone in the crowd said to Jesus, "Teacher, tell my brother to divide the inheritance with me." Jesus replied, "Watch out! Be on your guard against all kinds of greed, a man's life does not consist in the abundance of his possessions."

And then Jesus told the people this story: "The land of a certain rich man produced a good crop. So he thought to himself, 'What shall I do? I have no place to store my crops.' Then the rich man said, 'This is what I'll do, I will tear down my barns and build bigger ones, and there I will store all my grain and my goods. And I'll say to myself, 'You have plenty of good things laid up for many years. Take life easy; eat, drink, and be merry.' But God said to the man, 'You fool! This very night your life will be demanded from you. Then who will get what you have prepared for yourself?'" Then Jesus said, "This is how it will be with anyone who stores up things for himself but is not rich toward God."

Another time Jesus was teaching his disciples and a group of people called Pharisees who loved money were listening. When they heard the words of Jesus they began to sneer and make fun of him. Jesus said to them, "You are the ones who justify yourselves in the eyes of men, but God knows your hearts. What is highly valued among men is detestable in God's sight" (Luke 16:15).

Then Jesus told this story: "There was a certain rich man who was dressed in the finest purple cloth and fine linen. He lived in luxury every day. At his gate each day was laid a beggar named Lazarus who was covered with sores and who longed to eat whatever scraps of food fell from the rich man's table. Dogs came and licked poor Lazarus' sores.

The time came when the beggar died and the angels carried him to Abraham's side. The rich man also died and was buried. In the place of the dead, where he was already in torment, he looked up and saw Abraham far away, with the beggar Lazarus by his side. So the rich man called to him, 'Father Abraham, have pity on me and send Lazarus to dip the tip of his finger in water and cool my tongue, because I am in agony in this fire.'

But Abraham replied, 'Son, remember that in your lifetime you received your good things, while Lazarus received bad things. But now Lazarus is comforted here and you are in agony. And besides all this, between us and you is fixed a great chasm, so that those who want to go from here to you cannot, nor can anyone cross over from there to us.'

Then the rich man answered, 'Then I beg you, father Abraham, please send Lazarus to my own father's house, for I have five brothers. Let Lazarus warn them, so they will not also come to this place of torment.'

Abraham replied, 'Your brothers have Moses and the Prophets; let your brothers listen to the Prophets' words of warning.'

'No, father Abraham,' the rich man begged, 'but if someone from the dead goes to my brothers, they will repent.' Abraham again replied, 'If your brothers do not listen to the words of Moses and the Prophets, they will not be convinced, even if someone rises from the dead.'"

A prophet named Zechariah spoke about the dead as prisoners in the waterless pit (Zechariah 9:11). The Bible speaks about the presence of water as giving life. The Holy Spirit that Jesus promised to send from God is that life-giving water (John 7:38-39).

For those who choose to live apart from God and without being mindful of God's blessing in their lives can only look forward to a 'waterless' future where one in great torment and thirst longs to have even one drop of water to cool their parched tongue.

———

*So he called to him, "Father Abraham, have pity on me and send Lazarus to dip the tip of his finger in water and cool my tongue, because I am in agony in this fire"* (Luke 16:24).

*Just as man is destined to die once, and after that to face judgment, so Christ was sacrificed once to take away the sins of many people; and he will appear a second time, not to bear sin, but to bring salvation to those who are waiting for him* (Hebrews 9:27-28).

# WATER STORIES

## 22. Jesus Thirsted so That We Might Freely Drink

*Bible Reference:* Exodus 3:8; Deuteronomy 11:14-15; 2 Chronicles 7:13-14; Psalm 69:21; Isaiah 53; Jeremiah 31:9; Matthew 27:34; Luke 22:20; John 4:14; 6:35; 7:37; 19:28-30, 34

In the stories of God's people in the part of the Bible called the Old Testament the land that God was giving to Abraham and his descendants was said to be a land "flowing with milk and honey." God had promised to provide abundant water in due season so the crops would be plentiful. Because the Israelites were also shepherds, there would be water for their flocks and green grass for the animals. When their King Solomon built the new temple as a place to worship God, he prayed for the nation and its people. Then God appeared to Solomon in a dream and said: "When I shut up the heavens so that there is no rain, or command the locusts to devour the land or send a plague among my people, who are called by my name, if my people, who are called by my name will humble themselves and pray and seek my face and turn from their wicked ways, then will I hear from heaven and will forgive their sin and will heal their land" (*2 Chronicles 7:13-14*).

God knew the people would soon forget and would stumble into sin and God's judgment would swiftly follow. When this happened and the people went into exile as their punishment, in due time God brought the people back to the land of promise. Through the prophet Jeremiah God said, "I will bring them back. They will come with weeping; they will pray as I bring them back. I will lead them beside streams of water on a level path where they will not stumble..." (*Jeremiah 31:9*).

God had a plan for his Anointed One to come who would be despised and rejected by his own people. He was to take upon himself their infirmities and carry their sorrows. He would be stricken by God and his body pierced for their sins and ours, his punishment would bring peace, for by his wounds sinners would be healed.

He would be put to death like a criminal and buried among the rich. But his body would not decay in the grave for he would be raised to life again and would return to the Father in heaven. In doing this he would pour out his life unto death, the innocent suffering for the guilty.

A prophet said about God's Anointed One, "They put gall in my food and gave me vinegar for my thirst" (*Psalm 69:21*).

On the night before Jesus was crucified he met with his disciples for a special meal. It was the time when the Jewish people remembered how God's angel had spared their lives in Egypt, by passing over their houses marked with the blood of a lamb. As Jesus ate with his disciples he took the cup of drink made from grapes and said to the disciples, "Drink from it, all of you. This is my blood of the covenant, which is poured out for many for the forgiveness of sins" (*Matthew 27:27-28*).

Later that night Jesus was arrested and tried, accused of saying he was the Son of God, which he was. For this Jesus was sentenced to death by crucifixion—to be nailed to a wooden cross and hung up to suffer and die of thirst and exhaustion. At the place of execution Jesus was offered a drink of wine mixed with gall as a drug to deaden the pain. But when he had tasted it, he would not drink it.

After removing his clothing, soldiers nailed Jesus through his hands and feet to a wooden cross and crucified him between two criminals just like the prophet had said. Jesus prayed for his enemies asking God to forgive them.

Later that day It became very dark and Jesus cried out in a loud voice, "My God, why have you forsaken me?" It was the time when Jesus took upon himself the sins of the people—the innocent suffering for the guilty. God accepted Jesus' sacrifice. After Jesus had cried out, "It is finished!" he said, "I am thirsty."

One of the soldiers who had crucified Jesus put a sponge on a reed and filled it with vinegar and put it to Jesus' lips. When Jesus had tasted from the sponge, he said, "Father, into your hands I give my spirit," and bowed his head and died. Later a soldier took his spear and pierced the side of Jesus bringing a sudden flow of blood and water from the wound.

During his ministry Jesus told many listeners that he had living water to give. He said, "If a man is thirsty, let him come to me and drink" (*John 7:37*). And again Jesus had said to the woman at the well, "Whoever drinks the water I give him will never thirst. The water I give him will become in him a spring of water bubbling up to eternal life" (*John 4:14*). And again, "He who believes in me will never be thirsty" (*John 6:35b*).

Because of Jesus' thirst on the cross, we may drink deeply and freely of his salvation leading to eternal life. In the old days God had punished His people when they sinned by withholding the rains so the land was dry and the people became thirsty. Now God in his mercy was offering an abundant pardon for sin and an abundant flow of living water for cleansing and quenching the thirst of sinners. In these stories that river of life giving water has flowed your way. It is yours to drink.

— — —

*"Later, knowing that all was now completed, and so that the Scripture would be fulfilled, Jesus said, 'I am thirsty.'*
*A jar of wine vinegar was there, so they soaked a sponge in it, put the sponge on a stalk of the hyssop plant, and lifted it to Jesus' lips.*
*When he had received the drink, Jesus said, 'It is finished.' With that, he bowed his head and gave up his spirit"* (John19:28-30).

# WATER STORIES

## 23. Here Is Water, Why Shouldn't I Be Baptized?

*Bible Reference:* Acts 2:17, 21, 32-33, 37-38; 8:26-39

After Jesus returned to heaven, his followers continued to tell the story of Jesus' suffering, death and resurrection from the dead. Soon after God sent the Holy Spirit to fill the followers of Jesus, one of the disciples of Jesus who was named Peter spoke to the people about the prophecies regarding the Messiah in God's Word. Peter said: "In the last days God would pour out his Spirit on the people....And everyone who calls on the name of the Lord would be saved" (*Acts 2:17, 21*). Then Peter told how Jesus, after his suffering and death, was exalted to the right hand of God in heaven.

When the people heard Peter's words they were cut to the heart and cried out to Peter and the other apostles, "Brothers, what must we do to be saved?"

Peter replied, "Repent and be baptized, everyone of you, in the name of Jesus Christ so that your sins may be forgiven."

Later Peter, filled with the Holy Spirit, was speaking to the people when he said, "Salvation is found in no other name under heaven given to men by which we may be saved" (*Acts 4:12*).

Another follower of Jesus named Philip became an evangelist, traveling about proclaiming Christ and performing miraculous deeds. An angel of the LORD said to Philip, "Go to the desert road that goes from Jerusalem to the coast." On the way Philip met an Ethiopian official who was in charge of the treasury of the queen. The man had gone to Jerusalem to worship God and was on his way home sitting in his chariot reading the words of Isaiah the prophet. These are the words he was reading:

*"He was led like a sheep to the slaughter, and as a lamb before his shearers is silent, so he did not open his mouth. In his humiliation he was deprived of justice....For his life was taken from the earth"* (Isaiah 53:7-8).

The official asked Philip, "Tell me, please, who is the prophet talking about, himself or someone else?"

Then Philip began with that very Scripture and told the official the good news about Jesus and how he had suffered and died for the sins of the people.

As Philip and the official traveled along the road in the chariot they came to some water. The official said to Philip. "Look, here is water. Why shouldn't I be baptized?" So the official ordered the chariot to stop. Then both Philip and the official went down into the water and Philip baptized him. When they came up out of the water the Spirit of the LORD suddenly took Philip away, and the official did not see him again, but went on his way rejoicing.

Jesus instructed his disciples that as they went into all nations they should make disciples of the people, baptizing them in the name of God the Father, the Son and the Holy Spirit, and teach them to obey all things that Jesus commanded. And Jesus promised to be with them, even until the end of the age (*Matthew 28:19-20*).

———

*Then Philip ran up to the chariot and heard the man reading Isaiah the prophet. "Do you understand what you are reading?" Philip asked* (Acts 8:30).
*When the people heard this, they were cut to the heart and said to Peter and the other apostles, "Brothers, what shall we do?"*
*Peter replied, "Repent and be baptized, every one of you, in the name of Jesus Christ for the forgiveness of your sins. And you will receive the gift of the Holy Spirit"* (Acts 2:37-38).

# WATER STORIES

## 24. The Crystal River of Water

*Bible Reference:* Psalm 1:1-3; 46:4; Isaiah 49:6; Ezekiel 47:1-12; Joel 2:28-29, 32; 3:18; Zechariah 13:1; 14:8a; Revelation 21:6; 22:1-5, 17

A prophet named Joel speaking about the Day of the LORD said:

*"I will pour out my Spirit on all people. Your sons and daughters will prophesy, your old men will dream dreams, and young men see visions. Even on my servants, both men and women, I will pour out my Spirit in those days...And everyone who calls on the name of the LORD will be saved"* (Joel 2:28-29).

In the Bible God's Spirit is often spoken of like water to be poured out on people, a drink to refresh and revive weary people, a river to flow freely and abundantly so anyone who desires may drink and be filled.

The psalmist pictured a righteous man as one who is nourished like a tree growing by the river. Here is what he said:

*"Blessed is the man who does not walk in the counsel of the wicked or stand in the way of sinners or sit in the seat of mockers. But his delight is in the law of the LORD, and on his law he meditates day and night. He is like a tree planted by streams of water, which yields its fruit in season and whose leaf does not wither. Whatever he does prospers"* (Psalm 1:1-3).

The psalmist also told of a river in the city of God, a stream to make glad the city, the holy place where the Most High dwells.

Speaking of the future, another prophet named Zechariah said: "On that a day a fountain will be opened to the house of David and the inhabitants of Jerusalem to cleanse them sin and impurity" (*Zechariah 13:1*). And, "On that day living water will flow out from Jerusalem, half to the eastern sea and half to the western sea, in summer and winter" (*Zechariah 14:8a*).

And still another prophet named Ezekiel adds to the story from his vision:

*"I saw water coming out from under the threshold of the temple and flowing toward the east. A man with a measuring line in his hand led me through water that was ankle-deep. He measured off a distance and led me through water that was now flowing knee-deep. Again he measured off a distance and led me through water that was waist deep. After measuring off still another distance the water was now too deep to cross, because the water had risen and was deep enough to swim in—a river no one could cross. Then the man led me back to the bank of the river. When I arrived there, I saw a great number of trees on each side of the river.*

*"The man said to me, 'Where the river flows into the Sea the water becomes fresh. Swarms of living creatures will live wherever the river flows. There will be large numbers of fish, because this water flows there and makes the salt water fresh; so where the river flows everything will live....Fruit trees of all kinds will grow on both banks of the river. Their leaves will never wither, nor their fruit fail. Every month they will bear, because the water from the temple sanctuary flows to them. Their fruit will serve for food and their leaves for healing'"* (Ezekiel 47:1-12).

The last book of the Bible continues the story of the river. In a vision John tells of future events when the Lord Jesus has returned to judge the living and the dead. For those whose names are written in the Book of Life a new heaven and earth is prepared. In his vision John says:

*"An angel showed me the river of the water of life, as clear as crystal, flowing from the throne of God, and of the Lamb, down the middle of the great street of the city. On each side*

88

of the river stood the tree of life, bearing twelve crops of fruit, yielding its fruit every month. And the leaves of the tree are for the healing of the nations. The throne of God and of the Lamb will be in the city. There those who serve him will see his face and his name will be upon them. There will be no more night, for the Lord God will give them light...." (Revelation 22:1-5).

Jesus told the people in that day, "Ask of me and I will give you living water."

The Bible story closes with an invitation to all: "To him who is thirsty, I will give to drink from the spring of the water of life." The Spirit of God says, "Come! Whoever is thirsty, let him come; and whoever wishes, let him take the free gift of the water of life" (*Revelation 22:17*).

# WATER STORIES

## Telling the Stories

The team has gathered to begin the water project. Local people are gathering to watch. There is interest and curiosity in what is going to happen. Soon the work gets underway. For sinking a tube well the pace is monotonous as the pipe is lifted and dropped, again and again. There is not much new to see after a few minutes. Now is the time for the Bible storyer to begin by asking some sensitizing questions related to water:

—Has anyone been really thirsty?
—Were you able to get water to drink?
—Have you thought about where the water in the ground comes from? Who made it?
—Have you ever been caught in a flood?

Think about some questions that would stir interest or give a focus to the story you plan to tell. If listeners respond, let them talk. It is great if several get into a conversation or get a good "buzz" going.

Mention or briefly explain that the stories you would like to tell come from the Bible. You know some stories that mention water, thirst, drought and rains, and bathing. Let's begin with a story about water in the beginning... Tell the first story. Take time with the story. Use some gestures as movement attracts and focuses attention. Walk around in the work area as you tell the stories.

When you finish the story, signal that it is finished by saying: That is the end of the story from God's Word. It is not always appropriate to lead a dialog or discussion related to the story. Whether you can or cannot will depend on the size of the group and their readiness to participate. The post-story discussion questions are a resource from which to pick and choose, and not to be followed slavishly.

91

Develop your own questions from the stories. If listeners don't readily respond to any of the questions, move on to another story. Don't try to explain the story unless there are questions from the listeners. Post-story discussion questions focus on story facts or major happenings, on how the listeners might relate to the story, and if there is some application or truth learned from a story that should be applied to one's life. Always be aware that listeners may hear something in the story that you missed or that is important to them.

If there is little or no interest, finish the story you had started and then get a group together among the work team or sponsoring families and story to them. Those who profess not to be interested can still hear the stories and not feel that the stories are targeting them. If this is not possible, then wait until evening or a rest time when the work team is sitting around and perhaps some of the local people are nearby watching the group. Begin a story here. Tell it to the work group, but loudly enough so that those who "aren't listening" can also hear it.

If listeners respond well to certain stories, these may be repeated again. Among oral communicators many enjoy hearing things that they are already familiar with. "So tell it again, Sam!"

It may be that some in the group are interested in learning the stories. So begin a training group where the stories are told and the listeners then repeat the stories. If listeners can't readily retell a story, either repeat the story or start the story and ask the listeners to help tell it by each contributing to the story. Make it a game.

Most likely in a setting like this the listeners might not be challenged to make a profession of faith from the closure stories. Be prepared in case there is interest and response. Otherwise consider the stories as pre-evangelism to be followed later by a more thorough set of stories that teach the truths leading to salvation rather than focusing on a theme alone.

The list of stories is given as a resource. Tell as many or as few as needed. Add other Bible stories as needed. There was not an attempt in this set to provide bridging between stories. Each story is provided as somewhat of a standalone story though some do have carryover.

These stories could be mingled with other story sets if used during disaster response or other relief ministries like for famine. There is now a set of *The Food Stories* to accompany this set.

In most situations an interpreter will be required. It is good to go over the stories with the interpreter or even to have English story copies to give the interpreter in case they need to make notes or look in their Bibles to see how best to express parts of the story.

If possible think about having the stories translated or worked up directly from local Bibles and recorded. The recorded stories could be played over and over during the water project duration.

Incidentally, not all water projects require long periods of time to complete. Some of the water sand filters with ultraviolet light initially used in Cambodia were brought in as a unit, set up and demonstrated. More recent filter designs are ceramic filters that fit over water containers that are distributed. In Myanmar low-cost water filters are made from rice straw and sold to villagers. In cases of short time frames or brief encounters when distributing the filters, choose a few stories to tell while the work continues or people are available. Again, if the distribution/installation team remains over an evening this is an excellent time to gather a story listening group.

Pray asking God to open listeners' hearts to the stories. Prepare for the storying session by learning the stories, if not verbatim, at least well enough so that the stories can be told freely without having to constantly look at either your Bible or a story book. Don't be afraid of making mistakes or leaving something out—you probably will! Just keep going and finish the story. If you feel that too much was omitted, tell the listeners that you left something out that is important so you want to tell the story again.

Bible story pictures can be useful in drawing attention to a story. For a group, all pictures should be 13x17 inches or larger. Some of the pictures from Global Recording Network like the "Look, Listen & Live" series display really well as the pictures are bold line drawings that are brightly colored. Be aware that some pictures can offend and so should always be tested before public use. For more information on finding existing picture sets, write me at jot2@sbcglobal.net.

If there are other questions related to any of the stories or how to use them in ministry, please feel free to write me at the above address. If you do use the stories or this theme concept, I would enjoy hearing from you to find out what worked or didn't work and to know how the stories were told—think of it as a mini-case study. This kind of feedback is helpful to me as a trainer to stay abreast of what is working and how it is working and if there are issues needing to be addressed in future Bible Storying resources.

For information on water filters like those being manufactured and used in Cambodia visit their website at http://www.rdic.org/home.htm.

# The Story of the Village Pump

Following is a delightful story of a rusty pump that gave dirty water in a village. Various attempts by the villagers are made to improve the appearance of the pump, to chastise it, to coax it through flowery speeches, until after all efforts fail to improve the water, the village medic's son volunteers that the water is dirty because of what is in the well. He descends into the well to clean it. Then the water is pure. The story is an allegory of the heart and the need for cleansing by the Savior. Villagers love this story and want to hear it every time. The story could be used as a conclusion to draw the net for decisions.

The original posters depicted pumps and settings familiar to Thailand. Once when I had used the posters as I told the story of *The Village Pump* in a village in Orissa, India, the people listened attentively. After I finished one of the men said: "That was a good story but our pumps don't look like that!" So it may be well to tell the story without the posters so the listeners can imagine that the pump in the story looks like their pumps and so relates to them.

This is a common occurrence among oral peoples who often cannot distance themselves from specific things in pictures that are different or unfamiliar in order to see the illustrated teaching.

The original posters and script came from Kannok Bannasan (OMF) in Bangkok.

## THE VILLAGE PUMP

**Note:** This story will enable you to show your listeners the foolishness of thinking that it is possible to be a really moral upright person (good works of righteousness) without experiencing a change of heart. Jesus said that it is out of the heart that evil things come (*Mark 7:21ff*); so it is the heart that has to be made new.

In telling this story it is strongly recommended that you use the Bible to back up what you say. People need to know

that what we are saying is God's Word and not just something we have thought up. The Holy Spirit can use His Word like a sword to pierce the hearts of listeners.
Now the story:

The inhabitants of a small country village were assembled in the local coffee shop to discuss what has to be done. Their great problem was that the village pump always gave dirty water that was completely unusable for washing, cooking, or drinking. The water was dirty and smelly. "It's terrible," they said. "Whatever shall we do? We can't go on walking far to get clean water."

Grandfather had an idea. "Look," he said, "we've been using this pump for the last ten years and now it's getting rusty and is badly in need of cleaning and a new coat of paint. A can of paint and a bit of hard work will soon solve the problem. We'll clean and paint the pump and then it will give pure water."

So saying, Grandfather went off to the general store and bought the best quality white paint they had. After carefully scraping off the rust with a wire brush he gave the old pump two coats of white paint. It looked splendid! Everyone came to admire his handiwork and were most loud in their assertions that this would surely solve the problem. A *beautiful* pump should *surely* give nice water. But alas! When they pumped up the water it was just as dirty and smelly as ever!

Another meeting was called and this time it was Uncle who took the floor. "Leave this to me," he said. "I know just what is needed. At meetings we speak good words so that people will be happy and feel good. Perhaps the pump is unhappy. It needs to hear some beautiful words." He then strode out to where the pump stood still gleaming from its fresh coat of white paint.

Uncle was a wonderful speaker. Because he was fluent everyone enjoyed hearing him tell stories or give advice in village meetings. He stood before the pump, opened his book, and for thirty minutes told the pump exactly what it ought to do. The listening villagers nodded their heads in approval. This was Uncle at his very best they said, nudging

96

each other with delight. If anyone could make the pump do its job then it was Uncle. But when he had finished speaking and stepped back, one of the young fellows pumped up the water, it was as black and smelly as ever. Everyone was disappointed. Some people were scratching their head and wondering what to do next.

So back to the coffee shop they all gathered. "What can we do now?" someone asked. "We've painted the pump and talked to the pump, and yet the water is no different at all." "I'm used to this," said the village teacher suddenly. "What we need do is to show the pump that if it refuses to give us clean water, then it will be punished. When my students misbehave in school I take my rod and severely discipline them. A good beating always makes the students behave and do what is right."

So the teacher took up a bamboo stick that was lying in a corner of the coffee shop and went out to the pump. "Now then," he said, "we put you here to give us good water. If you don't, you will be punished. What do you have to say about that?" Since there was no response from the pump, the teacher laid into it with his stick until some of the new paint came off and the stick was broken into pieces. "There," he said, "it should have learned its lesson now." But again when the villagers pumped up the water there was no improvement at all — just the same dirty smelly water as usual!

The atmosphere in the coffee shop was quiet. No one could think of what to do. They had tried everything. People were just sitting around looking at one another and shaking their head. Just then the village medic spoke up. "The problem," he said, "comes from inside, not outside. The problem is in the well, not in the pump."

So the medic took his son to the well and removed the cover. Then the medic let his son down to the bottom of the well on a rope. The son collected the rubbish that had accumulated in the well over the years and put it all in a bucket which his father then hauled to the top. As they collected many bucketfuls, all sorts of things came to light—a dead cat, old rusty cans, a rubber tire, a bicycle frame, a pair of old shoes, and a number of broken bottles. When the son had collected all the rubbish, his father pulled him up out of the well.

After replacing the cover on top of the well, the medic pumped up the water. And this time it was clear and clean! There was no bad smell! There was no bad taste! What rejoicing there was! Now the people could drink and use the water once more. The problem had been inside the well, not outside in the pump.

----------

Throughout history human beings have sought ways to make themselves more acceptable to God. Many go on pilgrimages, some torture or beat themselves, or fast, or become monks who live a severe lifestyle. Yet the problem remains. Jesus said: "The good man brings good things out of the good stored up in his heart, and the evil man brings evil things out of the evil stored in his heart. For out of the overflow of the heart his mouth speaks" (*Luke 6:45*).

Jesus called the crowd to him and said: "Listen and understand. What goes into a man's mouth does not make him unclean, but what comes out of his mouth, that is what makes him unclean" (*Matthew 15:10-11*).

"Don't you see? The things that come out of the mouth come from the heart, and these make a man unclean. For out of the heart come evil thoughts, murder, adultery, sexual immorality, theft, false testimony, slander. These are what make a man unclean (*Matthew 15:16-20*).

God has sent the Holy Spirit to descend into our hearts and point out what makes us unclean. We cannot make ourselves clean by our own works. We open our hearts to God's Holy Spirit when we believe that Jesus, God's righteous Son, received our punishment and died in our place. We ask for God's forgiveness for our sin and believe in Jesus as our Savior. When our sins are forgiven God's Holy Spirit cleanses our hearts so that what now comes forth is clean and pure and pleasing to God.

Is your heart like that well in our story? Have you tried to make your heart clean and right? Would you permit your heart to be cleaned God's way? Then it will be pure again.

## Suggested Scriptures to Use When Applying the Story:

*1. Society is basically wicked.* This is why there is so much stealing, lying, cheating, hatred, murder, anger, greed, lust and unhappiness (*Ephesians 2:1-3*).

*2. Individually we are wicked.* This is the reason we cannot be the kind of people we know we ought to be or would like to be (*Mark 7:21ff*).

*3. Those who try to clean up their hearts by observing various religious rites or by engaging in various forms of good works* (*Matthew 23:25-28*).

*4. Those who feel that preaching and telling men what to do is the answer* (*Romans 7:14ff*).

*5. Those who feel that threatening with punishment in the future will help* (*Romans 1:32*).

*6. The Christian answer*:

**Regeneration:** John 3:3

**A new heart:** 2 Corinthians 5:17

**Free forgiveness:** Ephesians 1:7

**The Holy Spirit within:** Acts 5:32

**An intercessor in heaven:** Hebrews 7:25

www.ingramcontent.com/pod-product-compliance
Lightning Source LLC
Chambersburg PA
CBHW052137090426

42741CB00009B/2117